The Digest Enthusiast

Book Four   **June 2016**

Cover		RK based on a photo by Mart— images.com
	2	Editor's Notes
Review	4	H.G. W——
Interview	8	Dig—
Fiction	16	A Ra— —ardi
Article	20	Suspen—
Index	39	Suspens— —eprint Sources
Article	41	Suspense
Review	49	*Bulldog Drummond* by Sapper
Fiction	52	The Hideout by Ron Fortier, Art: Rob Davis
Article	62	The Galaxy Science Fiction Novels by Steve Carper
Review	79	*Mystery, Detective, and Espionage Magazines* by Michael L. Cook
Interview	82	Art Taylor
Article	96	The Galaxy Magabooks by Gary Lovisi
Article	100	Criswell Predicts: *Fate* & *Spaceway* by Tom Brinkmann
Fiction	120	Strangers in Need story and art by Joe Wehrle, Jr.
Synopses	125	*Shock Mystery Tales* by Peter Enfantino
Fiction	134	Wounded Wizard by John Kuharik, Art: Michael Neno
Article	146	*Pocket Pin-ups* Trading Cards by Max Allan Collins
	148	Social Intercourse
	151	Opening Lines

Editor/Publisher/Designer Richard Krauss   Contributing Editor D. Blake Werts
Cartoons by Brad Foster and Bob Vojtko

Visit us online at larquepress.com/blog for current and vintage digest covers and news. Join our privacy-secure mailing list, used exclusively for updates on *The Digest Enthusiast* and Larque Press at larquepress.com

---

The Digest Enthusiast (TDE) Book Four, June 2016. © 2016. Contributors retain copyright of content contributed. TDE aspires to quarterly publication by Larque Press LLC, 6327 SW Capitol Highway, Suite C #293, Portland, Oregon 97239. All rights reserved. Unauthorized reproduction in any manner, other than excerpts in fair use, is prohibited.

Note: Scanned covers that appear in TDE are retouched to remove tears or other defects from the original source. When reference material is not available, retouched areas are "best guess."

Editor's Notes

Is the tail wagging the dog? In this hybrid age of print and digital editions, readers make trade-offs they may not be aware of. The EPUB format is based on html and only supports a single column. Not a big problem for the books it was designed for. Magazines are another story. For most of them, page designs with multiple columns are an important part of the reading experience. But they have to be reworked for EPUB. And graphics require far more space than text, so graphics in magazines are often trimmed back for EPUB to lessen the download penalty.

There are alternate formats like Zinio, but like Kindle, they are proprietary. PDF seamlessly carries the print design, but is so prevalent, it's a tough choice if you want any control over distribution.

Pulps and digests have traditionally featured two-column layouts. The short line lengths were ideal for their fast-paced stories. Unfortunately, most popular fiction digest magazines today are designed with a single column. The only exception being *Analog*. Single columns make the conversion to EPUB format much easier, but for me makes the print versions far less inviting to read.

The experts have long advised 39 characters (an alphabet and a half) as the ideal line length for readability. I chose four lines at random from the latest editions I had on hand and averaged them.

Here are the characters per line:
Analog: 44
F&SF: 74
AHMM: 75
EQMM: 76
Asimov's: 83

From a visual perspective, *Analog* is clearly the most inviting to read, and *Asimov's* the least. I was surprised that *F&SF* came in virtually identical to the mystery books. However, with its smaller page size and more generous leading I'd still argue that *F&SF* is more inviting to read than the rest of the single-column crowd. And I should mention that *Fate* also continues to print with a two-column format. Thank you, Phyllis Galde.

As Alec Cizak says in our piece on digital digests, "They have yet to invent a program that translates a PDF directly to Kindle format."

I'm pleased to say that all of the esteemed contributors in this edition have returned from earlier issues with new offerings. Plus Sean Azzopardi and Rob Davis join the fun with their wonderful illustrations for our two crime fiction stories.

Steve Carper provides a detailed review and history of Galaxy Novels, that's complemented by Gary Lovisi's piece on their short-lived Magabook two-fer series.

Tom Brinkmann's article on The Amazing Criswell offers a fascinating look at the seer and his prognostications, but also demonstrates how

Editor's Notes

the joys of research can open doors and take a writer in new directions.

The contents of *TDE* slowly gels as an issue nears deadline. Peter Enfantino had signed on for a look at the *Weird Tales* digests, but found he had too much on his plate already. Instead, he brings us a sobering look at *Shock Mystery Tales*, a title that sounds as if it's more fun to read *about* than to actually read. Hopefully, we'll pin him down on *Weird Tales* for next time.

Our fiction includes a nice mix of fantasy, science fiction and crime stories by Ron Fortier, John Kuharik, Gary Lovisi and Joe Wehrle, Jr. with artwork by, respectively, Rob Davis, Michael Neno, Sean Azzopardi, and Joe himself.

Joe is always full of surprises. He's introduced me to another digest I'd never heard of before, with his review of the *H.G. Wells Society Newsletter*.

Articles and features don't always end at the bottom of a page, so there is often space for a cartoon, a plug or some other short item to balance out the page. Brad Foster calls them "fillos." A short, sweet description that fits. I'm grateful to Brad and gag cartoonist Bob Vojtko for their "fillos" that add a welcome resbit on every page on which their work appears.

For myself, I offer a few digest reviews, uncover a classic GGA digest trading card set, and report on one of my favorite reference volumes by Michael L. Cook. My piece on *Suspense Magazine* and its spin-off Suspense Novel series was great fun to research and write. Plus award-winner Art Taylor provides an issue highlight with a terrific interview.

Let's get started.

-RK

The following retailers stock *The Digest Enthusiast* on their shelves along with a wonderful selection of other great books, pulps and comics. My thanks to Mike and Greg for your support.

Mike Chomko
sites.google.com/site/mikechomko-books/

DreamHaven Books & Comics
2301 E 38th Street
Minneapolis, MN 55406-3015
(612) 823-6161
dreamhavenbooks.com

SALT SHAKER EXPLORING SPACE

©brad w. foster. 2009

H.G. Wells Society Newsletter Issue 30
Review by Joe Wehrle, Jr.

This may be a somewhat unusual entry in the catalog of digest-size publications, but I think the newly-redesigned *H. G. Wells Society Newsletter* certainly qualifies for inclusion. I recently received issue 30, Autumn 2015, with cover illustration by J. Begg, reproduced from the *Illustrated London News* of 25 January 1913. The art, obviously inspired by Wells' book, *Little Wars*, published about the same time, depicts the author seated on the floor amid toy soldiers, model houses and small fortresses. Wells and Robert Louis Stevenson are said to have actively played these war games with their sons. Near the end of his book, Wells tells us, "You have only to play Little Wars three or four times to realize what a blundering thing Great War must be."

I find articles in the Wells Society publications to be very carefully researched and highly literate. A majority of the writers and the editorial staff have doctorates and associations with prestigious universities. They tend to delve deeply into the subject matter, avoiding superficiality and the stereotypical.

Eric L. Fitch, secretary for the Society, has written "H. G. Wells, Windsor and Me," which is, in part, a personal remembrance for Eric, but also a chronicle of Wells' times in Windsor, and of how descriptions of the area often turned up in his novels. And we learn that a hotel in the district often served as a rendezvous for Wells and Rebecca West during their affair!

H. G. WELLS SOCIETY NEWSLETTER

Autumn 2015
Issue 30

Editor: Dr Maxim Shadurski

ISSN 2059-6391

Robert B. Cronkhite's "Interpretation of Our Sun in Future Time in *The Time Machine* by H. G. Wells," discusses how Wells' description of Earth in the very distant future corresponds with what science has learned since the time of his writing. This interpretation is a response to the article by Mary V. Mills in an earlier issue, and theories of Stephen Hawking are referenced.

Patrick Parrinder reviews *The Housekeeper's Tale: The Women Who Really Ran The English Country House*, by Tessa Boase, which is a group biography of five British housekeepers, interesting to Wells readers because his mother, Sarah, is one of the subjects. In his autobiography, Wells states that his mother was "perhaps the worst housekeeper that was ever thought of." Nevertheless, five volumes of Sarah's diaries exist, and appear to furnish a valuable record of her times, the existing customs, and the nature of the duties which occupied her life until young Wells' literary success enabled him to settle her in a comfortable cottage for the rest of her life. Most serious readers of Wells know that the first section of *Tono-Bungay* is very autobiographical (hilarious at points), and paints a vivid picture of the British estate system.

In 1978 Jeff Wayne created, as a double album, *A Musical Version of The War of the Worlds*. James Smith writes of the performance tour Wayne has embarked upon in recent years, with additional musicians, a 3-D hologram of Liam Neeson as H. G. Wells interacting with the live performers, and a thirty-foot Martian fighting machine which descends upon the stage mid-performance, spitting fire above the heads of the audience.

Events and announcements pertinent to the Society are reported, including details about the forthcoming conference in July 2016, and memorials are written for recently-deceased members.

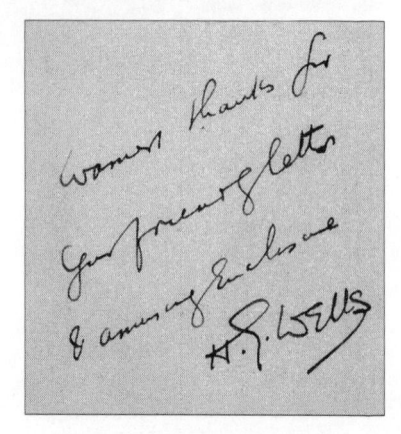

This newsletter is issued twice a year, and there is also a thicker, and very scholarly annual, *The Wellsian*.

The H. G. Wells Society was formed in 1960, and currently has members in over twenty countries. It aims to promote "widespread interest in the life, work and thought of Herbert George Wells."

The Society's web pages can be accessed at hgwellssociety.com.

Subscriptions and general enquiries may be addressed to secretary Eric L. Fitch, 20, Upper Field Close, Hereford HR2 7SW, UK.

Digital Digest Magazines
Compiled by Richard Krauss

As print on demand and EPUB digital technologies created the self-publishing phenomena, a smaller, new wave of digest magazines also appeared, and seem to be gaining traction. Several editors of leading titles share their experiences and challenges.

Digital printing equipment offers a wide variety of formats, but the papers and cover stocks compatible with the technology and its ecomonics, limits the selection. Digital book publishers can choose from many trim sizes, but most opt for 6" x 9" (trade paperback-size) or slightly smaller, aka digest-size. This 2:3 ratio is ideal for looks and comfort.

Some of the new digital digests appeal to a specific interest like *The Digest Enthusiast* or *Monster!*, with primarily nonfiction content. But the grand tradition of titles like

Manhunt and *Galaxy* have inspired a new crop of editors and publishers to start their own fiction magazines.

Pulp Modern was an early entry. Editor Alec Cizak explains, "Initially, I started *Pulp Modern* because I didn't see a lot of print journals that published good, interesting fiction in a variety of genres. With the absence of a lot of crime fiction journals today, I've switched the focus to crime fiction only (which would have happened regardless since the majority of submissions I've always received at *Pulp Modern* have been crime fiction)."

Rather than specialize, Jennifer Landels, editor of *Pulp Literature*, went the other route. "We felt there was a gap in the market for well-written multi-genre stories. Literary magazines tend to ignore genre fiction, and other fiction platforms tend to be narrowly genre-specific. We wanted to create a smorgasbord where all genres are welcome, and the only criteria are good writing and good storytelling."

Adam Bradley and Stanley Riiks' love of horror, fantasy and SF began when they were youngsters. Their early publishing efforts, *Violent Spectre* and *Black Tears* were produced on a photocopier. Later, their popular Myspace page drew over 24,000 followers. "And it just grew from there. We originally printed the [*Morpheus Tales*] magazine ourselves, but moved to print on demand [POD] because of the costs of production and shipping (we're based in the UK, whereas most of our readers and contributors are US-based). We've been doing digital editions of the magazine since the third issue because it's easy to set up and you can sell unlimited amounts. We sold out of most of our early issues before moving to POD."

John Kenyon was another early entrant with *Grift*. "I started *Grift* because at the time there were few print venues for crime fiction. Plenty of online outlets, but the opportunities to publish in print were lacking, I thought. At the same time, the sensibilities of the publications that did exist—both in print and online—seemed at odds with what I and others I knew liked to read and write. While it seemed as if other publications leaned toward the ultra-violent, I wanted something more cerebral. No less hard-hitting, but just with less gore. I also wanted to offer a forum for nonfiction

Kristen Valentine's *Betty Fedora* #1

work, independent scholarship that would help to expand readers' understanding of the genre."

Kristen Valentine, began her title *Betty Fedora*, "Because the other crime fiction magazines out there, while very good, feature stories that are heavy in the noir tradition: men getting in fights, femme fatales, and that's it. I wanted to explore stories featuring female characters as a starting point."

Although technology makes these low- and no-budget magazines possible, they share many of the same challenges as a traditional publisher. "Money is the biggest problem," Bradley and Riiks confirm. "When we launched we threw some money at *Morpheus Tales*, we paid some high profile authors, we spent money on advertising in the top genre magazines like *Interzone, Cemetery Dance*, etc. for the first year or so to try to get some momentum."

For Bradley and Riiks it eventually became too difficult to find the time required to publish a digest magazine. After much soul-searching they decided it best to hand over the editorship to someone else who could continue the tradition of *Morpheus Tales*, but also take it in new directions. That was when current editor, Sheri White, stepped in.

Grift's Kenyon finds lack of time the biggest obstacle. "The long-gestating third issue of *Grift* is delayed because I simply don't have enough hours in the day. Also, a lack of funding that would allow me to pay beyond contributors copies. You get what you pay for, and my ability to get the type of nonfiction I desire has certainly been compromised by that."

Money was also an issue for *Pulp Literature*'s Landels, but she took a unique approach to the problem. "We ran a Kickstarter campaign to launch the magazine which, though successful, was an extraordinary amount of work. We ran a second one for our next year, and then started up a Patreon page to generate ongoing funding, though we're still operating off loans. Marketing and subscription sales are the most challenging part of running the magazine."

The surge in self-publishing also created a surge in writers. Keeping pace with submissions is big job for a fiction magazine editor. *Betty Fedora*'s Valentine has learned to streamline the process. "We accepted submissions via email for our first two issues, which wound up being somewhat difficult to manage logistically (lots of forwarding, downloading, etc). For our third issue (which will be available later this year), we have transitioned into using Submittable, and that is making it easier."

Still, for many fiction magazine editors submissions require the majority of their time. "Yes, reading submissions and deciding which stories to publish—always a tough choice," says Valentine. "The actual design and production of the magazine is pretty easy (it helps that I'm a designer in the real world)."

For *Morpheus Tales*' White, "Proofing and editing the chosen stories takes longer than choosing the actual stories. It can be interesting correcting errors in a story, depending on whether the author is American or not, because there are different terms and slang used here that aren't used in the UK. Sometimes I have to Google a term or word I'm not familiar with to make sure it's being used correctly. Spelling can be tricky as well; for instance, 'color' and 'colour.'

"Writing the editorial can be difficult, because I'm not sure if what I say is going to appeal to everyone since I'm an American writing for a UK-based magazine read by horror lovers from around the world."

"In general, we try to allocate about one third of our time to marketing and sales, one third to production, and one third to editing," says *Pulp Literature*'s Landels. "In reality we have the production end of things running pretty smoothly. Editorial goes up and down depending on submissions' openings and issues' deadlines, and marketing time is what suffers when we're short on hours."

"Unfortunately, what most

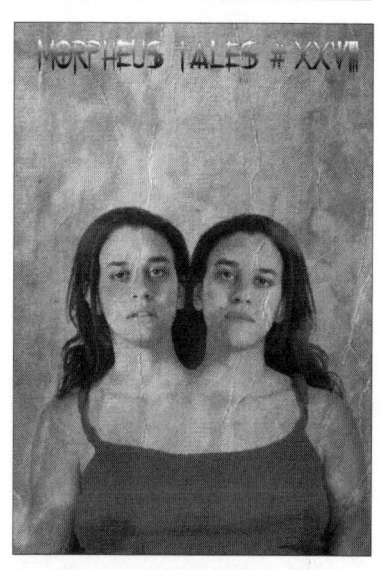

Sheri White's *Morpheus Tales* #28

occupies my time is not doing the magazine," says *Grift*'s Kenyon. "When I do have time, it's taken up by soliciting submissions, reading them and selecting the stories we'll publish. Editing that work takes some time, and then doing my own writing, which has been the major hang-up in this latest issue. In the absence of nonfiction submissions, I still have plenty that I want to write, but lack the time to do it."

Every issue of each magazine requires promotion to let potential readers know it's available now. When *TDE* launched I ran ads for three months in the classified sections of each of the major newsstand fiction digests. Correlating response from those ads was difficult because there were also concurrent announcements on PulpComingAttractions.com and several news and review blogs, but it's fair to conclude (and unfortunate) sales did not offset the expense.

Pulp Modern's Cizak relies

John Kenyon's *Grift* #2

on social media. "I use Twitter and Facebook and encourage the contributors to promote the journal any way they can." *Betty Fedora*'s Valentine echoes the point, "It's always a bit of a struggle just launching a brand new project and getting people to pay attention, but our writers and readers have been wonderful about helping to spread the word." She adds, "When we released Issue 2, we ran a promotion on Issue 1 to be free for the first week. We got a lot of downloads from that, and I think this may have contributed to the consistent level of sales we've been seeing ever since. Issue 2 definitely has sold many times more copies than our debut, although Issue 1 is still selling as well."

Girft's Kenyon agrees, "We try to have a strong social media presence, though like everything else, that is compromised by time. Word of mouth in the crime fiction community is the best tool. That's certainly where I hear about things, and what I hear typically drives my decision to purchase or not."

"Social media, reviews, and listings in submission trackers like Duotrope are all very helpful," reports Landels of *Pulp Literature*. "Our contests always generate a spike of interest as well. However, in-person appearances at conventions and conferences tend to be the most effective activity. When people are able to flip through print copies at our tables they are wowed by the look and feel, and usually start reading on the spot."

"Social media is good at raising awareness, but as Facebook continues to drive businesses towards the paid advertising model it becomes more and more difficult to reach followers without spending money," advises *Morpheus Tales*' White. "There are still organizations that promote genre work, like the British Fantasy Society and others, that help. And the small press is a community, people are friendly and happy to help get the word out there."

Series titles have the advantage of multiple issues, so publishers may choose to offer a free sample. White has found, "Free previews really help give readers an idea of what they're getting. All of our issues have free previews, and we also offer some magazines for free."

Once they connect, all of the publishers have found their readers receptive. As White says, "We have a small core readership which has grown over the years, they buy every magazine and love it. The response we get from people who see the magazine is always positive, although we're more well known for the incredible artwork than the stories, perhaps because those images are used to market *Morpheus Tales* in a different way to the stories. The difficulty is growing the readership. We have a whole new audience because of the digital editions, and can reach places we wouldn't be able to via print."

Valentine says reader support for *Betty Fedora* is fantastic. "Especially with our second issue, things are really starting to take off. It's thrilling that readers were also hungry for a women-focused crime fiction magazine. The main comment we get is to the effect of 'We definitely need more female characters,' which is always awesome to hear."

Landels' experience with *Pulp Literature*'s reader response is very positive. "We get rave reviews from our readers, who really appreciate the variety and quality of stories as well as the design and art. We just need to get the word out to more of them."

"Those who have read the journal [*Pulp Modern*] are generally enthusiastic," says Cizak. "The few reviews the journal has received have been positive." Contributors too, "are always enthusiastic."

White's experience with *Morpheus Tales* is similar. "Contributors love the magazine. We have so many regular writers and artists that it really feels like a team. Since we've moved to POD the cost of contributor copies has increased significantly and we've had to reduce the number, so writers no longer received a printed contributor copy (only digital). This has definitely impacted the number of submissions we receive."

At *Pulp Literature*, editor Landels has found, "Authors appreciate the editorial time we take. Each piece

Alec Cizak's *Pulp Modern* #10

goes through story edits, copy edits, and final proofreading, so its very clean by the time it hits the printed page. Some stories come to us almost ready to print, while others take quite a few hours of structural work. We're willing to put that work in if the story is a diamond in the rough with a sparkling plot or unique voice. And writers love it when their stories get illustrations."

For Kenyon, *Grift*'s prolonged publishing cycle can be tough on contributors. "They seem to like it when they actually get to see it. They understandably don't appreciate the long wait between acceptance and publication." That said, *Grift* is an outstanding title. As a reader, I'm willing to wait as long as Kenyon keeps issues coming.

Contributor response for *Betty Fedora* has also been terrific. "We get submissions from published authors with novels to their names, as well as brand new writers," says Valentine.

Jennifer Landels' *Pulp Literature* #10

"We're very happy to be involved in a writer's career at any stage."

The mix of print to EPUB sales varies by title. *TDE* readers prefer print over Kindle about 3:1 which I attribute to most of our audience being collectors as well as readers, who want to see an issue on their bookshelf. Landels of *Pulp Literature* puts her average ratio at about 70% print, 30% digital.

For *Morpheus Tales*, White estimates her readership at about 50/50. "I think digital sales continue to grow, and we've built a large back catalogue of issues which continues to sell, which doesn't get so much attention in print, unless we do special offers, which we do regularly. Print seems to need to be pushed, digital sales just seem to come in steadily."

The electronic version always sells more than the print version of *Pulp Modern*. "I've tried to make the price of the print version close enough to the electronic that the average person would say, 'Well, might as well spend two more dollars and have a real book in my hands,'" says Cizak. "But it doesn't work that way. The general population is sold on the e-book thing and, apparently, prefers them to real books." That's true for *Betty Fedora* as well, where Valentine reports at least 95% of sales are Kindle.

Today, *Grift* is only available in print. But Kenyon is willing to change that. "I'm always thinking about offering a digital version to allow more people to read this work. The writing is on the, um, screen, and I'm sure we'll start doing print and digital soon."

Every version adds incremental sales, but many editors like Kenyon, Cizak and myself prefer print copies. And for a few of us like *Morpheus Tales'* White, print is the only option. "I still don't own a kindle or e-reader, so it's always been important to print a proper book or magazine. To hold something in your hands that you've created is a much more visceral experience than holding a digital edition on a device. But I know as a publisher you have to explore as many options as possible to get your content into the hands of the reader, whether that be print, digital or something else."

"Print reading is a different experience from digital," says Landels of *Pulp Literature*. "My biggest joy in the production process is getting the print proof in the mail. Even though I've read those stories several times by that point, it's incredible how much more I enjoy reading them on the printed page. (I also manage to catch typos that have escaped five sets of proofing eyes, including my own, in the digital form)."

"Even though we live in the future," says *Betty Fedora*'s Valentine, "not everyone uses an e-reader, and I wanted to make the magazine available to everyone. Plus, I wanted to be able to share a print copy with contributors."

Like Valentine, my background is design, so creating multiple versions of *TDE* has simply become part of the production process. Although it's important to note that the print version allows much greater flexibility in the design than EPUB—particularly in regards to graphics and fonts. However, you can add color to an EPUB at no cost whereas in print, interior color will likely double your costs.

Valentine adds, "We publish our digital version for Kindle only so we really just have two versions (print and EPUB). The Kindle version is more time consuming for me than the print version is, since e-readers are notoriously finicky about formatting. I do the print layout first since there is additional production time for ordering and reviewing a printed proof. While that's being created, I make sure the Kindle version is in good shape. Coordinating them both to be available at the same time is probably the biggest challenge."

Pulp Modern's Cizak is not a designer. "Creating the e-book is a pain in the ass. They have yet to invent a program that translates a PDF directly to Kindle format. For the last two issues I've hired people on Fiver to format the book for me. There's no clickable table of contents, but the integrity of the print version is intact."

"The preparation for the POD and digital editions is very similar," says *Morpheus Tales*' White.

"The amazing artwork unfortunately only appears in the print editions of the magazine. That's because the file sizes are just not supported digitally, that's a shame because the artwork really adds to the impact of the story."

Pulp Literature leverages every sales channel. "Along with print, we make html, PDF, EPUB and mobi versions, all of which are available when you buy the digital issue," says Landels. "It took us a while to find the right eBook formatter, so the EPUB and mobi versions of issues 1–3 are not quite what we wanted. However, by issue 4 we found Booknook.biz and they are absolutely fabulous: fast, accurate, and great people to work with. They use the InDesign files supplied by our designer and the ebooks look as close to the print version as possible given the format. However, I still feel that to appreciate the graphics, e-subscribers would do well to check out the html or PDF versions as well as downloading the ebooks for their readers."

I think it's fair to say that today's new wave of POD/digital digests remain more a labor of love than profitable business venture. Some offer small payments to their contributors, while others can only provide contributor copies. Every editor expresses appreciation to their readers for their support. The single biggest compliment you can pay a magazine publisher is to continue purchasing issues of their title. And if you really want to go the extra mile, tell your friends. Each magazine will only get better as their readership grows.

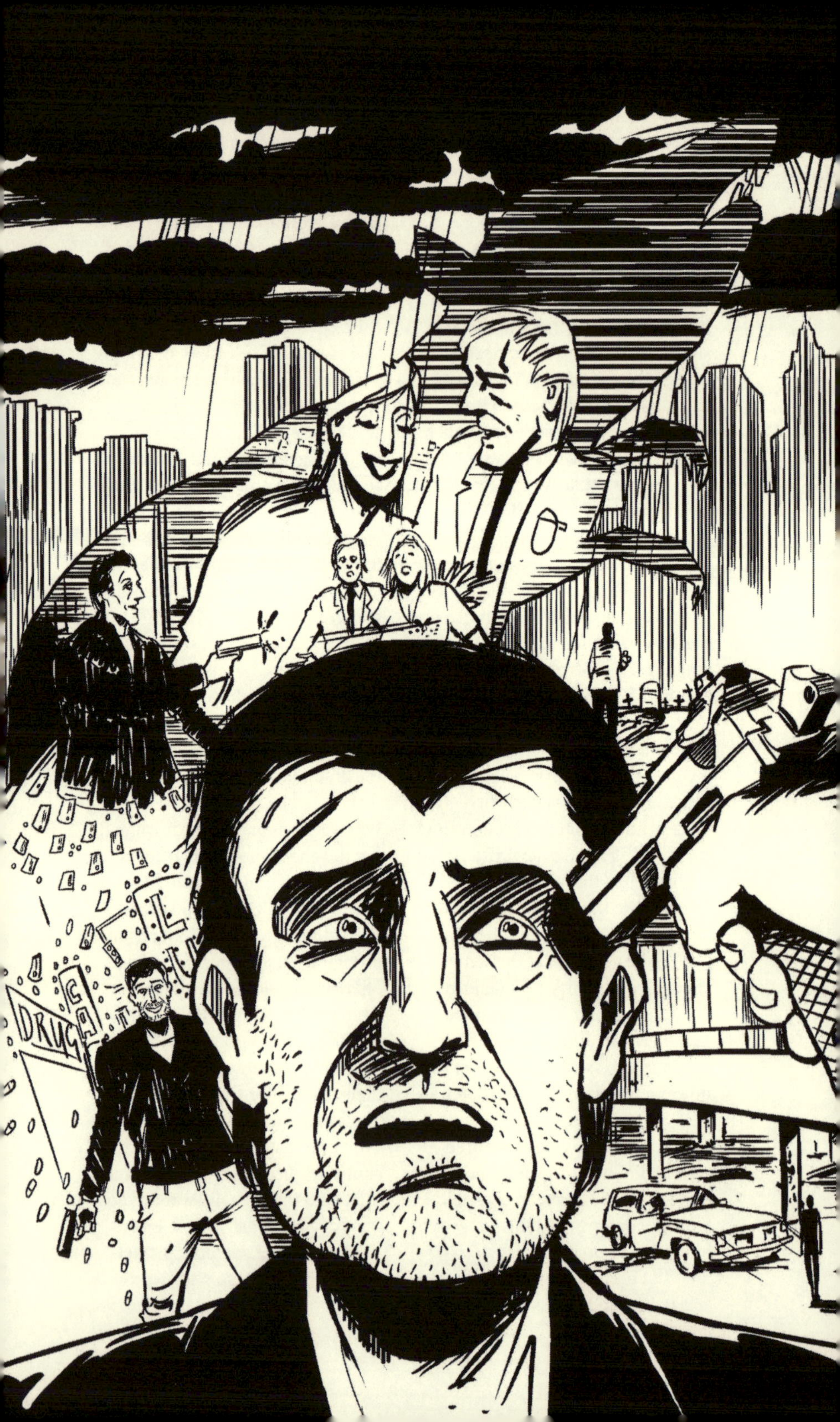
DRUG

A Rat Must Chew

Crime fiction by Gary Lovisi
Illustration by Sean Azzopardi

You're about to enter the world of Vic Powers. Hardboiled, violent, and unrelenting, Powers metes out justice on his own twisted terms. Kicked off the force for excessive brutality, whatever controls were holding him back were cleanly severed. Now he's free to track, hunt and convict any lowlife foolish enough to become his target.

Jimmy Dongen was a Staten Island wiseguy with his dirty hands into more dirty crap than even he could keep track of. Anything and everything to make a buck and not just gambling and other soft vices, but nasty stuff like teenage hookers, drug dealing in schools, selling guns to kiddie gangs. The guys under Jimmy saw him as a greedy fuck, the guys over him saw him as a greedy fuck who brought in the cash. He was a good earner so they all put up with Jimmy Dongen while he tried his best to smart-ass double-cross them all when they weren't looking. He figured he'd end up with everything he ever wanted.

I don't think he even knew all of what he wanted—he just wanted.

My name is Vic Powers. I came into it originally back in the old days when I'd been on the job. Before they threw me off the force for being "unstable." Hell, I wasn't unstable, I was just damn angry that a lowlife creep had killed my partner, Larry, and I wanted to do something about it. Larry was the best damn friend I ever had. The best damn cop I ever knew. Damn right I was angry. I was fit to be tied! But I wasn't unstable, least ways any more unstable than I'd ever been. But then again, I guess I could see their point, and it probably all worked out for the best. I wasn't cut out to be a cop. Not the kind of cops they want. Yes-men, ass-kissers, sell outs and politically correct rats—a lot of them no better than the criminals they're supposed to arrest.

Well, all that was a lot of water under the bridge now, but over the years Jimmy Dongen had moved up, turning into one of the biggest of the bad guys. But he'd made a lot of enemies along the way.

He told me once long ago, after I'd saved his ass, that he wanted to go straight.

I told him he was full of shit.

He had acted all serious about it back then.

I just looked at him and said, "Rats must chew, that's just the way it is, Jimmy".

He got all upset, thought I was calling him a rat.

I smiled, said, "No, Jimmy, you're not a rat. Least far as I know, you're not. You're a scumbag, but you ain't no rat."

There is a difference.

Then I told him that to live a rat must chew. Rats—the four-legged kind, that is—have huge incisors that keep growing in their mouths and if the rat doesn't constantly gnaw at things, constantly chew, cut and grind with those teeth to wear them down, the damn teeth will grow right into the rats brain and kill it.

"Nice way for a rat to die," Jimmy had said.

"It's like that with a scumbag like you, Jimmy. You'll never stop. You'll never go straight. It's in the blood. Rats must chew and scumbags like you will never stop what they do."

Then Larry and I cuffed him and brought him in.

Well, that had been a long time ago. Like they say, a lot of water under the bridge, a lot of blood too. Now Larry was gone and I was on my own.

Now I was a two-bit no-one in a world that had dreamed me out of its dreams a long time ago. So I did the next best thing, I hung in and survived. I did my best to make it day to day. Trying to beat the odds but coming up craps with every throw. In the meantime I never dared to hope.

It was after Larry had been killed, but before my wife, Gayle, had been murdered. That's how I usually remember events in my life, I date them from who it was, who was close to me—and when they were taken away from me. Killings, murders, my partner, Larry, my friends, my women, my enemies, my wife. . .

Anyway, Gayle was still alive back then and we were trying to have a real life. I was playing the hubby and loving it. Thinking of opening an office again, maybe a husband and wife P.I. team? A dream I shouldn't have let enter my mind.

Then Jimmy Dongen entered my world again.

He was on the run.

The cops—crooked and otherwise, the mob, a Jersey biker gang that dealt drugs, an upstate Aryan Separatist group that paid Jimmy a lot of good money for some very bad guns. They were all after Jimmy and I was in Jimmy's car parked under the West Side Highway while he was telling me all this crap.

I said, "Why, man? You had it good; you could have stopped the crap, taken it easy. You play so many games, so many sides against each other you were bound one day to get caught in the middle."

"I know, Vic," he said. "I guess it had to happen sooner or later. You know how it is. I got to do what I do. I can't stop. I could never stop. Once I started a life of crime, Vic, once I started playing The Game, I just couldn't stop it. I love it too much. Now I know there's only one end for us all, eventually."

"You know all this shit and you still fuck around."

"Yeah, I know all this shit, and it doesn't help me by knowing it."

"Not if you don't do anything to stop it, Jimmy."

He smiled, "A rat must chew, Vic."

I nodded.

The gun slipped into my hand.

I pressed it up against Jimmy's temple.

Jimmy's eyes blew up into big circles of surprise, and then understanding.

It was quick.

I pressed the trigger.

One.

Two.

He fell away from me.

I wiped the gun and placed it in his right hand, melding the fingers to the grip. Opened the door. Locked the passenger side as I got out of the car and walked away.

A rat must chew.

This was one rat that would never chew again.

Gary Lovisi is an author, also a bookseller and collector who writes about collectable paperbacks. Under his Gryphon Books imprint, he publishes *Paperback Parade*, the world's leading magazine on collectable paperbacks of all kinds. You can find out more about him and his work at his website: gryphonbooks.com

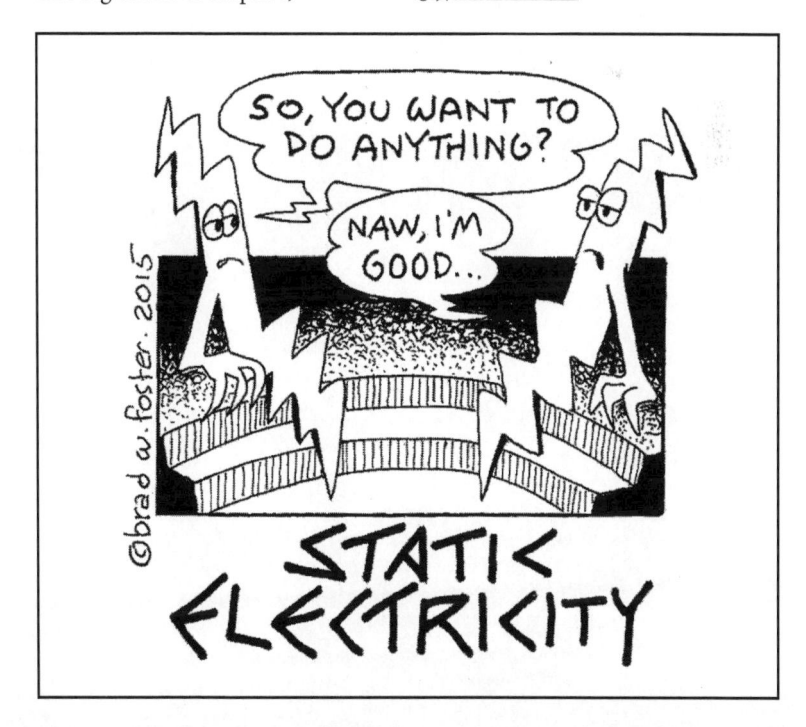

SCIENCE FICTION • MYSTERY • CRIME • FANTASY

SUSPENSE

HIGH-TENSION STORIES

THIRTY FIVE CENTS

SPRING 1951

JOHN DICKSON CARR	●	HONEYMOON TERROR
RAY BRADBURY	●	SMALL ASSASSIN
WILLIAM TENN	●	THE QUICK AND THE BOMB
A. B. SHIFFRIN	●	A MOST AMAZING MURDER
JOHN GEARON	●	FACES TURNED AGAINST HIM

PLUS other startling SUSPENSE stories by Theodore Sturgeon, S. Fowler Wright, James A. Kirch, Peter Phillips, William Hope Hodgson, Alex Samalman, John Chapman and Oliver Saari.

Suspense Magazine #1 Spring 1951

Suspense Magazine
Article and synopses by Richard Krauss

"The first issue of *Suspense Magazine* relied more on reprints than original material, but this formula was reversed in subsequent editions. Theodore Irwin was editor for all four issues."

CBS radio ran a programing experiment during the summer of 1940. *Forecast* presented a series of back-to-back, diverse half-hour radio shows to gauge listener response. The winners: *Duffy's Tavern* and *Suspense*—the latter for its adaptation of Marie Belloc Lowndes' 1913 novelette "The Lodger," directed by Alfred Hitchcock.

The *Suspense* radio program began as a series in the summer of 1942, produced and directed by Charles Vanda for the first six episodes. William Spier took over as producer on episode seven, and sometimes director of the program, for the next several years. Over his career Spier wrote, produced and directed for radio and television. He directed *Lady Possessed* for Republic Pictures in 1951. A year later he produced the first season of *Omnibus* for CBS television.

Spier won a Mystery Writers of America award in 1947

Ellery Queen's Mystery Magazine Sept. 1944

Ellery Queen's Mystery Magazine Sept. 1945

for *The Adventures of Sam Spade* and a Writers Guild of America award in 1962 for a two-part script for *The Untouchables*.

Bernard Herrmann was chief conductor at CBS radio for seventeen years, beginning in 1934, writing and conducting for many CBS radio programs, including *Suspense*. He wrote the *Suspense* theme and also wrote and conducted music for many of the program's early episodes.

The series narrator, the "Man in Black," originally Joseph Kearns, was first named on the January 12, 1943 broadcast that featured an adaptation of Edgar Allan Poe's "The Pit and the Pendulum," starring Henry Hull. The adaptation was scripted by John Dickson Carr.

Carr joined the program in 1942 and wrote many of its scripts, including adaptations of his own stories. Carr's script for one of the program's most popular episodes, "Cabin B-13" (episode 33, March 16, 1943) was printed in *Ellery Queen's Mystery Magazine* (May 1944).

Actor Sydney Greenstreet played Carr's Dr. Gideon Fell in "The Hangman Won't Wait," which aired on February 9, 1943. That script was later published in *EQMM* (September 1944), marking ". . . the first Dr. Gideon Fell radio story ever to appear in print."

Another of Carr's scripts, sans Dr. Fell, "Will You Walk Into My Parlor?" (episode 30, February 23, 1943), ran in *EQMM* (September 1945).

Unfortunately, Carr left the program over a creative dispute. In June 1943, CBS censors objected to an Italian villain in Carr's "The Man Without a Body," thinking listeners might perceive an ethnic slur. They issued a mandate that criminals should be either American, British, Japanese or German. Carr refused to comply and left CBS in anger to work for the BBC. When his script aired on June 22, 1943, the villain was German.

Carr ramped up quickly at

the BBC, writing new scripts for stories he had used on *Suspense*, and by September 1943 *Appointment With Fear* debuted, which might be considered a British knock-off of *Suspense*.

The Lone Wolf made his radio debut on *Suspense* on July 20, 1943 in "Murder Goes for a Swim" adapted from a novel by Louis Joseph Vance. *Suspense* often adapted the work of mystery and crime fiction writers, including Dashiell Hammett, Agatha Christie, Dorothy L. Sayers, Ben Hecht, Cecil Day Lewis (Nicholas Blake) and Richard Connell, to name a few. But the author whose stories were most often adapted was Cornell Woolrich, whose stories appeared 31 times during the radio show's 21-year run.

Suspense the Mystery Magazine #1 Nov. 1946

Television

Auto-Lite brought *Suspense* to television in March 1949 on CBS. The first episode was "Revenge" written by Cornell Woolrich, starring Eddie Albert and Margo (Albert). CBS aired 260 episodes over a six-year run, of which only 90 survive. Early broadcasts relied on adaptations of the radio scripts, including "Suspicion," "Cabin B-13" and "Dead Ernest." But soon original scripts were produced including an early Rod Serling effort, "Nightmare at Ground Zero." The final episode in 1954, was "Barn Burning," based on a William Faulker story, scripted by Gore Vidal.

Two years after the radio program ended in 1962, CBS launched a television reboot, hosted by Sebastian Cabot, but this final effort lasted less than a full season.

Comic Book

There was also a *Suspense* comic book, initially published by Cornell Publishing and distributed by Marvel Comics, which debuted in December 1949. The first two covers featured movie stills: *The Verdict* with Sydney Greenstreet, Peter Lorre and Joan Lorring (issue #1), and *Abandoned* with Dennis O'Keefe and Gale Storm (issue #2).

A cover blurb: "Dangerous Adventure–Mysteries Wired for High Tension — Based on Gripping CBS Radio–Television Series" appeared on issues #1–11, and was then dropped for the remainder of the comic book's 29-issue run.

The Suspense Digests

Two different digest magazines were published based on the *Suspense* radio program. Each had four issues. The first re-presented short story adapta-

The Woman with Woman's Digest Sept. 1945

Everybody's Digest Vol 7 #1 Jan. 1948

tions of radio scripts. *Suspense the Mystery Magazine* was edited by Leslie Charteris and CBS agreed to license the magazine only if they chose the stories included. The 112-page monthly digest was based in Los Angeles and published from November 1946 to March 1947. Each cover featured the lead actors from the episodes adapted inside.

Michael L. Cook wrote in *Mystery, Detective, and Espionage Magazines*, "As a whole, the stories were rather shallow and, it is hoped, were more effective when heard on the air."

In 1951, the second digest affiliated with the program debuted. *Suspense Magazine*'s stories may have been inspired by the radio show it was named for, but their association with its scripts ended there. Published by Farrell Publishing, its president Tom Farrell held the copyright on its contents.

Farrell was the successful publisher behind *The Woman with Woman's Digest*. They maintained offices in Chicago at 350 East 22nd Street and editorial and executive offices in New York at 420 Lexington Avenue. From 1944 to 1950 *The Woman*'s editor was Dorothy Johnson, who also wrote short stories throughout her career. In 1953 her anthology, *Indian Country*, included "A Man Called Horse," brought to life onscreen in 1970 with Richard Harris. Another movie based on one of Johnson's stories was *The Man Who Shot Liberty Valance* (1962). In 1951, Lorna Farrell returned as editor of *The Woman* digest, a role she'd filled prior to Johnson's stint.

Tom Farrell was also president of W.J. Smith Publishing, which published *Everybody's Digest: Reading Matter That Really Matters*, under the editorial guidance of Theodore Irwin. The few issues of *The Woman* and *Everybody's Digest* that I've seen, reprinted or condensed versions of articles from other sources, although *The Woman* ran some original content.

Both magazines enjoyed wide

circulation during their early years. *Everybody's* reported 1,973,000 copies in annual newsstand circulation 1949, which dropped to 1,296,000 copies by 1953. Even more dramatic, *The Woman* reported 4,820,000 copies in 1945, which plummeted to 1,375,700 by 1952. Both Farrell and W.J. Smith Publishing filed voluntary petitions in bankruptcy on May 24, 1954.

Farrell also published at least a few books, including *The Man: An Anthology of the Best Articles of the Year for Men* (1940) and *The Working Press of the Nation* (1947). Farrell and W.J. Smith each published versions of Bill Wenzel's *The Flimsey Report* (circa 1953) a cartoon digest that satirized the *Kinsey Report*.

Arnold E. Abramson was vice-president under Farrell at Farrell Publishing and general manager at W.J. Smith Publishing. Later, as head of Universal Publishing and Distributing (UPD), Abramson launched *Ski Life* magazine in 1959, following the path of special-interest magazines. In 1969, UPD purchased *Galaxy Science Fiction*, which struggled until Abramson hired James Baen as editor. However, its rejuvenation didn't last long. When Baen left in 1977, it only added to the magazine's financial difficulties, from which it never recovered and ceased publication in 1979.

The second *Suspense* digest lasted no longer than the first, but it reportedly had a larger circulation. Its stories covered a wide swarth of genres, perhaps intended to maximize its appeal. The magazine's tagline, "High-Tension Stories," was the unifying theme the stories inside shared. A tiny line-art icon of a woman screaming in terror, exuding electric waves of shock was the "logo" that appeared on several covers and the publisher's promotional pages inside.

The *Suspense Magazine* "Logo"

The first issue of *Suspense Magazine* relied more on reprints than original material, but this formula was reversed in subsequent editions. Theodore Irwin was editor for all four issues. N.R. de Mexico, who will be covered in more detail later, began as associate editor (issue #1–3) and became managing editor (issue #4), replacing R.B. Williams. Arnold E. Abramson was general manager (issue #1 & 2), a position not listed in the credits after issue #2.

Suspense Magazine #1
Spring 1951

The Deathless Ones
by John Chapman and Oliver Saari ★★★

A monolithic space ship transports a crew of two thousand to colonize a new world light years away. Everything aboard the self-sufficient wonder goes exactly as planned until the crew and its expanding population realize the conditions in space have an unexpected effect on them—they are no longer aging and will expend their resources long before they reach their destination.

Voice in the Night
by William Hope Hodgson ★★★
The lone survivors of a shipwreck discover a strange fungus on a deserted island. A truly creepy story.

A Most Amazing Murder
by A.B. Shiffrin ★★★
The opening scene, depicted on the cover, shows a naked woman, laying on her bed with her throat cut. It's a serviceable yarn, told first person by the detective who solves the murder. A. (Abraham) B. Shiffrin was most famous for his broadway plays (*Love on Leave*, *Angel in the Pawnshop*, *I Like It Here*, *Twilight Walk* and *Black-Eyed Susan*); several were later produced for television. He also wrote novels (*The Other Cheek*, *Blind Men*, *Told Out of School*, *Glitter*, *Mr. Pirate*, and *Return at Sunset*) and numerous short stories.

Obviously Suicide
by S. Fowler Wright ★★★
A prolific author who wrote over a dozen science fiction, mystery and historical novels between 1924 through 1954, Wright also wrote under the names Sidney Fowler and Anthony Wingrave. At the time he wrote "Suicide" for *Suspense*, he was the magazine's senior contributor at age 70. It's not exactly science fiction—*Suspense* labels it a science-storyette (a short or shortened story)—in this case three pages. A researcher discovers a deadly combination of three commonplace substances, all easy to obtain, that could wipe out the earth in a matter of seconds.

The Eyewitness Who Wouldn't See by James A. Kitch ★★★★★
An issue highlight, "Eyewitness" concerns the owner of a diner and his girl. Both witness a murder, but only the girl is brave enough to make a statement. Before the case goes to trial, she disappears. The police and a gangster pressures the diner's owner to reveal the girl's hiding place. Problem is, he really doesn't know. A tight plot with good dialogue and mounting tension made this yarn well worth reprinting.

Small Assassin
by Ray Bradbury ★★
Great writing, but despite Bradbury's talent, I had a hard time getting past the story's premise of a new born bent on murder.

The Quick and the Bomb
by William Tenn ★★★★★
Tenn was the pseudonym writer Phillip Klass used for most of his

science fiction stories, reserving his own name for his nonfiction work. Born in the London, Klass grew up in Brooklyn, New York. After marriage, the couple moved to Pennsylvania, where he taught comparative literature at Penn State University. Among his students who became writers themselves were David Morrell and Ray Ring.

Tenn's stories appeared in *Astounding, Galaxy, F&SF* and many other magazines and collections. In "The Quick and the Bomb" a man rejects city life to build a self-sustaining bomb shelter under his farm to protect his family from the impending nuclear war. It's a fascinating glimpse into post-WWII anxieties, told with Tenn's trademark sarcastic wit.

She Didn't Bounce
by Peter Phillips ★★★★

A cocksure suitor, enamored with a plump woman in his office plays a cheeky game of seduction in a surprisingly ribald entry that runs just three pages. Phillips was a UK writer and journalist, with nearly two dozen science fiction and detective stories published in US pulps and digests. His most famous, at least at the time of *Suspense* #1, was "Manna," first published in the Feb. 1949 *Astounding* and "perennially reprinted in anthologies."

Jeannie and the Light Brown Cure
by Alexander Samalman ★★★★

The curative properties of music are amplified by the Dynamic Sound Ray Case in this light-hearted science-fictiony romp. Samalman was editor of *Thrilling Wonder Stories, Startling Stories* and several other titles for the Ned Pines publishing empire.

Ghost of a Chance
by Theodore Sturgeon ★★★★★

A jealous spirit plays havoc on behalf of his living object of affection on any and all males she may encounter casually or otherwise. The premise could have gone north or south, but in Sturgeon's capable hands it's a witty, engaging ghost story with a satisfying end.

Honeymoon Terror
by John Dickson Carr ★★★

Intro: "Numbering its audience in the millions today, the CBS radio-television program series *Suspense* for a number of years has ranked as one of the finest dramatic programs on the air. It has brought to perfection a new type of high-tension presentation—in tune with our time, in harmony with modern concepts of gripping entertainment.

"In each issue, the magazine *Suspense* will present one of the distinguished scripts which have made broadcasting history. The initial choice, Honeymoon Terror, was originally given over the CBS network in November, 1943, under the title Cabin B-13, starring Margo and Phillip Dorn."

"Cabin B-13" was one of the most popular episodes of *Suspense*, it was rerun in November 1943, but its original broadcast was in March of that year.

Faces Turned Against Him
by John Gearon ★★★★★

Gearon's fine novelette wraps up the first issue of *Suspense Magazine* on a high note. Gearon

hooks readers with his characters, action and the magazine's high-tension standard. Here's one of several nice passages:
"The windows were up and the heater was on. An hour after noon, cold weather had descended suddenly on New England. The road to Bridgeville and the county jail was like a ribbon of toothpaste squeezed snake-like across the dull brown landscape."

John Gearon wrote scripts for both the *Suspense* radio and television programs. Under the pseudonym John Flagg, he wrote a series of thrillers for Gold Medal Books in the 1950s, including *The Persian Cat*, which was recently reissued as Black Gat Book #4.

Suspense Magazine #2 Summer 1951

The cover illustration on issue #2 was a dramatic break in the visual style from *Suspense* #1. The image of a woman in peril remained a constant, but limited color palettes and use of line art likely set the magazine apart from its competition in 1951. The smaller figure of a man on the right is not immediately obvious, but if you look closely you'll see him.

Operation Peep
by John Wyndham ★★★

Perhaps most famous for penning *The Day of the Triffids*, Wyndham contributes a "science satire" as the opener for *Suspense* #2. People from an alternate universe are popping into ours at inopportune moments. The story never takes itself too seriously and indulges a few gems like this bit of scathing commentary on the world's stupidity:

"We've got two ways of using inventions," she said. "One is to kill more people more easily; the other is to help short-sighted goons make easy money out of suckers."

But don't worry, the hero saves the world from peeping eyes and gets the cynical beauty to boot.

Blood Will Tell
by Nathaniel Weyl ★★★★

A brief, but tightly-plotted short with murder, blackmail and revenge tangled together just like its cast of characters. Weyl (pronounced "while") was an economist and author of two books, *Treason* (1950) and *Red Star Over Cuba* (1962). In his youth, a member of the Communist Party of the United States (1933–1939), he later leaned conservative and became a vocal anti-communist. In 1952, he testified against Alger Hiss, a former State Department official, convicted of perjury, who served 44 months in prison. Weyl died in 2005 at the age of 94 in California.

The Nightmare Face
by Walter Snow ★★★★

A newspaper journalist and pulp fiction writer, Snow wrote mostly adventure and detective stories. *The Walter Snow Papers*, hosted by Thomas J. Dodd Research Center, reports: "Snow's writing style is characterized by his ability to bring his characters to life." Here's an example from this story:

"Carlotta flirts indiscriminately with eager sailors, pats their cheeks, blows them kisses. When they get too fresh she brandishes a baseball bat prankishly. It's an act that keeps the bar crowded when the fleet is

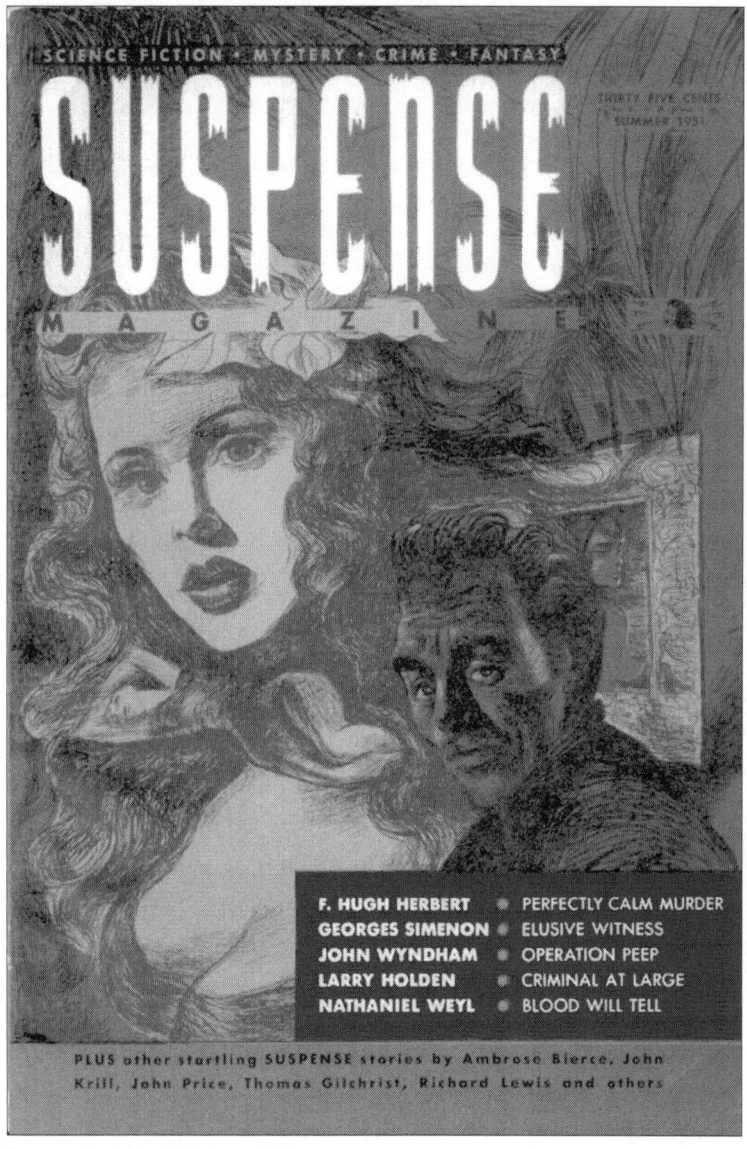

Suspense Magazine #2 Summer 1951

in. Brazenly, Carlotta sasses all her customers: 'You're stingy tippers. Me, I want a man with money.'"

Set in the Florida Keys, Carlotta's brazen behavior ends suddenly when she turns up dead beside her suspected paramour in the wake of a hurricane. It's up to local law enforcement to figure out if the storm had any help.

Snow's work also ran in *Gang World*, *Mike Shayne*, *Short Stories* and *Suspect Detective Stories*—and was anthologized in collections like *20 Great Tales of Murder* and *With Malice Towards All*. He wrote two mystery novels *The Golden Nightmare* (1952) and *The Gauguin Murders* (1972).

Survival
by Thomas Gilchrist ★★★★

Three men adrift in a dinghy after their boat capsizes at sea, fight for survival as heat, hunger and thirst draw them closer to death every moment. It's no surprise who maintains their humanity as desperation rises between the wealthy boatman, an old man and a native Pacific islander, but Gilchrist does a beautiful job describing the tension as their plight worsens.

Criminal at Large
by Lozenz Heller ★★★★

Heller was a novelist, short story writer and screenwriter who wrote dozens of shorts for detective magazines under the name Larry Holden from 1946 to 1959. "Criminal" sets up a tension-filled confrontation between a housewife and an escaped killer. Unlike many of the stereotypes in stories of this era, the housewife, Aunt Libby, could fend for herself: "She could fix anything. Last Spring, when the level-wind on my reel jammed, she fixed it in nothing flat, and still got more trout than Uncle Steve and me."

Elusive Witness
by Georges Simenon ★★★★★

Jules Maigret, or simply Maigret, was a French police detective who starred in 75 novels and 28 short stories. An invention of Georges Simenon, who was influenced by his long time friend, Chief Inspector Marcel Guillaume. Maigret was the subject of several television series around the world, three French films and a BBC radio series in the 1990s.

"Elusive Witness" is a fine murder mystery, with a choir boy as the only witness, and a complete lack of physical evidence. Before it's over Maigret manages to sleuth out the missing body and the murderer, despite the skeptics surrounding him.

Simenon was a master of his craft. Besides a first rate plot and fascinating characters, he slips in witty commentary like, "Old men, after all, are given to sulking like children; they are apt to have the same fits of waywardness."

Sick in bed with a cold or perhaps the flu, the detective's only comfort is the chance to ruminate on the murder, while his wife plays nursemaid to her cranky patient's waywardness. At one point she complains, "'You took your temperature only half an hour ago.' Just the same, she shook the thermometer to bring down the mercury and slipped it in where it would do the most good."

Beyond the action, it's this level of characterization that brings the story and its actors to life. Readers are privy to the fatherly warmth Maigret feels for the young witness, whose claims are easily dismissed by the patrolmen and the other adults of authority. A top-notch story.

Black Death
by John Krill ★★★★★

A first rate tale of revenge that pits an infamous matador against a bull named Black Death. The story opens with a spread by llustrator Ken Rice. Krill's stories appeared in *Black Mask*, *The Saint*,

15 Story Detective, *F.B.I Detective Stories* and *Exciting Detective*.

Fatal Mistake
by John Basye Price ★★★★

As a storyette (3 pages), "Mistake" must get to its point quickly. As such, it's not much more than a one-two punch. Set up the situation and deliver the unexpected ending.

Penny Wise, Fate Foolish by Mary Elizabeth Counselman ★★★★

Intro: "Once voted by readers the most popular short story ever printed in *Weird Tales*, where it appeared under the title "Three Marked Pennies," this closely knit fantasy is among the finest of the kind. Cited by the writer's magazines for excellence of plot, it has been dramatized for stage and radio, and reprinted in England, France, Denmark, Norway and Holland. Its most recent appearance was in the Rinehart collection *The Night Side*, edited by August Derleth."

Written when Counselman was a teen, "Penny Wise" is a macabre tale that sets its table stakes high: wealth, world travel or death. Where the game began is left a mystery, and its winners may not cash-in the way they expect.

Counselman went on write for *Collier's*, *The Saturday Evening Post*, *Good Housekeeping* and others, but her landmark story was one of the three all time most popular in *Weird Tales*' long history.

World Within
by Thomas A. Coffee ★★★★★

Billed as a science adventure, Coffee's story was a hoot. An investigator from the Board of Health soon finds myself at peril from a Dr. Cyclops-type threat. Their battle inside the clinic soon morphs into a fantastic voyage at the cellular level. It's a wild contest of wits and an exhilarating adventure ride.

Pardon My Terror
by Irving Burstiner ★★★★

Editor Theodore Irwin wrote that submissions often seem to arrive in trends. A wave of "wife murders or ghost yarns." For *Suspense* #2 there was a run on "fiends," from which Irwin selected two, based on merit and because ". . . they serve to emphasize the vast differences writers can bring to the same theme."

"Terror" is only just over three pages in length, yet Burstiner manages to add a clever twist to bring his story's fiend to a satisfying end.

Evil Is the Night
by Edith Saylor Abbot ★★★★

Like the previous story, the tension in "Evil" is built through the imagination of the reader. The fiend may or may not be on-scene, but his rep positively dominates the page. Here again, the final twist is unexpected and devastating.

Maiden Beware
by Richard Lewis ★★★★

This issue's radio script is the episode first broadcast on July 27, 1944 as "The Black Shawl." A young woman is hired as a private companion and soon finds herself fearing bondage and slavery. Is it just her nerves or is something seriously wrong with her employer?

The Perfectly Calm Murder
by F. Hugh Herbert ★★★★

A man who has just murdered

his much older wife, recounts how he came to the deed and where he slipped up in getting away with it. Herbert was a playwright and screenwriter. His play, *Kiss and Tell* ran on broadway, and was made into a film, starring Shirley Temple.

A Horseman in the Sky
by Ambrose Bierce ★★★★★

Bierce's stories feature wit, irony and a healthy dose of skepticism about the human condition. Perhaps his most famous short story "An Occurrence at Owl Creek Bridge" was first published in *The San Francisco Examiner*. Also the original source for this story, a fine example of the writer's talent exploring a favorite theme of his: war—in this case the American Civil War.

Suspense Magazine #3
Fall 1951

Suspense included only a few interior illustrations in each issue. Some are obvious page-fillers, while others are fully rendered works used to launch their stories. Don Rice was a near-regular, but unfortunately *Suspense*'s other artists didn't sign their work or I wasn't able to decipher their signatures.

The Saboteur
by William Sambrot ★★★★★

The third issue starts with a bang. Sambrot's tale of espionage and terrorism remains timely. His description of a terrorist organization, their methods and their targets strikes a chilling sense of familiarity nearly 70 years later.

My Favorite Corpse
by Dorothy F. Horton ★★★

This tightly constructed murder story serves justice to its perp swiftly, but with only three pages there wasn't much space to add depth.

Love Ethereal
by Horace L. Gold ★★★

The renowned editor of *Galaxy* conjures up a comedic farce in which a severely dysfunctional marriage is analyzed and alienated from beyond.

The Thing on the Snow
by Waldo Carlton Wright ★★★★

Categorized as "macabre," this story is every bit its label. It involves an elderly couple, hard winters on their farm and ghastly intentions gone horribly long. Wright's stories can also be found in *Alfred Hitchcock's Mystery Magazine* and *Mike Shayne*.

Dear Automaton
by A. E. van Vogt ★★★★

A story must be terrific to reprint it barely a year after its original appearance in *Other Worlds Science Stories*. This robots versus humans story adds some clever ideas to keep it interesting and above expectations.

Rip Tide by Russell Branch ★★★★

Branch apparently wrote more science fiction than crime, but he seems to have enjoyed adding a few poetic passages to this one, a murder mystery lurking just below the surface. Some of its passages call too much attention to the writing, but others are quite crisp: "Lora Walton took me like a slug of gin, on that hot empty afternoon."

Suspense Magazine #3 Fall 1951

Wall of Fear
by Will F. Jenkins ★★★★★

First published in *Collier's*, Jenkins used his given name for this story rather than his famous pseudonym Murray Leinster. It's an excellent story about an ex-con who made some rather foolish choices early on, and continues to live under their cloud.

You Can't Run Away
by Philip Weck ★★★★★

When a story starts strong

and keeps getting better, you can't help but stop for a moment to double-check who the writer is. It's a name you want to remember. For technique alone—wonderfully, smooth transitions from second to first person and back again—this story's a killer. A war veteran returns to his hometown and finds his perception of things has changed more than the people and the place. Except for the murder—and that changes everything.

With a little searching I was delighted to find Weck's stories appeared in dozens of pulps and digests from 1947–1961, including *Manhunt*, *Trapped*, and *Triple Detective*. I'm looking forward to reading more of his work.

Not a Leg to Stand On
by Don Mardick ★★★★★

Another five-star story. A prison break sparks an encounter between a cop, an insurance investigator and the escapee's brother. Loot, gunplay and a wheelchair add motivation, tension and considerable action. It's unfortunate there isn't more of Mardick's work available, the only other published story I could find was in *Hollywood Detective*, Dec. 1949.

Terror in the Sun
by Talmage Powell ★★★★★

At the other end of the spectrum, Talmage Powell wrote hundreds of stories for pulps and digests, including *Ellery Queen*, *Alfred Hitchcock*, *Mike Shayne* and *Manhunt*. "Terror" centers on a father's hunt for his son's killers in the sweltering heat of the Everglades. Armed with a shotgun, tension builds as the search progresses; exploding when he finds them.

How Can You Be Reading This?
by Charles H. Gesner ★★★★

A story built around a wacky job function—expungers—those tasked with erasing anyone they're sent to call on. Perhaps it was prophetic as this appears to be Gesner's only published work.

The Seventh Man by Sir Arthur T. Quiller-Couch ★★★★★

This beautifully written story features a team of six men trapped in an Arctic winter, trying to maintain order and sanity while they await the sun and its associated rescue. Quiller-Couch (1863–1944) was an English author, poet, anthologist and literary critic, also known as simply "Q." He held several public offices and advocated for reform of the English school system. He was Knighted in 1910.

Pattern for Dying
by Morris Cooper ★★★★

A revenge story—at least perceived revenge—in which an ex-con returns to his victim, whom he blames for his crime and his subsequent conviction.

Cooper's 20-year writing career includes work in numerous pulp magazines and single placements in the digests: *London Mystery*, *Edgar Wallace* and *The Saint*.

Dark Vengeance
by Fritz Leiber, Jr. ★★★★★

The cover story, "Vengeance," opens with another beautiful illustration by the same artist who drew the cover. Leiber's famed series characters Fafhrd and the Gray Mouser, star in this novelette about a powerful priestess who controls an army of black raptors.

Suspense Magazine #4 Winter 1952

Threat of Violence by R. J. Burrough ★★★

A school teacher wins $15,000 on a radio quiz show when she answers a nearly impossible question in Latin. Unfortunately, her good fortune does not go unnoticed. Here's the scene as she exits the theater: "Umbrellas opened to join the stream of bobbing black mushrooms gleaming under marquee lights. The avenue was bouncing with cold rain, splashing as taxis whooshed arrogantly by over oily pavements splotched with yellow and green."

This chaotic weather provides perfect cover for a small gang of watchers who grab the suddenly unlucky Miss Craig off the street and take her to their brownstone hideout. Fortunately, the teacher's wits win the day a second time before the tale's closing curtain.

The Screaming Woman by Ray Bradbury ★★★★

Despite the announcement in issue #1, there were no *Suspense* radio scripts presented in issue #3 or #4. Bradbury's piece here is a story, but it was first heard on radio (episode #316) as a script on November 25, 1948. The background on this popular story is conflicting. One source credits Sylvia Richards for adapting Bradbury's tale for radio, yet its first record as a published story was in the *Today* magazine of the *Philadelphia Inquirer* on May 27, 1951, almost three years later. A second source credits Bradbury with the original script for *Suspense*, that he later adapted for print in *Today*, which seems more chrono-logical.

A young girl, through a neatly arranged set of circumstances, seems to be the only living person to believe one of her neighbors has been buried alive. The story was dramatized for the EC comics line in *Crime SuspenStories* #15, Feb/Mar 1953 and featured on *The Ray Bradbury Theatre* on television, on Feb. 22, 1986, with Drew Barrymore. On January 29, 1972, it aired as the *ABC Movie of the Week*, starring Olivia De Havilland in the title role—transformed from youngster to a former mental patient—whom nobody believed either.

And Never Came Back by Dorothy Marie Davis ★★★★★

This cover story features a divorced woman and her daughter riding a train to a reunion with her ex-husband. Complicating matters is the second wife, also aboard, and a serious change of heart by hubby who now wants his ex and current wife to swap places. It may sound a bit forced, but Davis does such a fine job of characterization and storytelling, its one of the highlights of the issue. Davis wrote a handful of poems and short stories, starting in 1933, mostly for romance titles, a writing career that apparently ended with her story in *Suspense*.

The Third Degree by Charles Lenart ★★★

Lenart captures the patter of the hardboiled style beautifully, but

Suspense Magazine #4 Winter 1952

the surprise ending of his yarn was a bit too obvious. I found only one other story credited to him that appeared in *Detective Tales* (June 1951). If it's the same "Lenart" found online, his writing career moved to copywriting and he died in Chicago in 2010 after a successful career.

Ask No Quarter
by Duane Yarnell ★★★

The introduction reports: "He sold his first seven stories before turning 21, and his slicks, pulps and network shows are legion." Beyond *Suspense* Yarnell's stories appeared in *Five-Novels Magazine*, *Trapped*, *Detective Tales* and *Alfred Hitchcock's Mystery Magazine*. But his main body of work was centered on sports—from team sports to hunting and fishing. Even his *Suspense* story is really a boxing yarn, with a twist ending that likely helped him place it here.

Yarnell wrote novels too, primarily sporting stories, but his novel for Crest, *Mantrap* (1957), appears to be genuine crime fiction. The back cover copy, written by the publisher, tells readers the book "packs a wallop like Mickey Spillane."

Find the Witness
by Ted Stratton ★★★★

Ed Emshwiller produced a striking scratchboard-style illustration that depicts the story's witness watching a woman as she's thrust over the railing of a balcony by her murderer. It's a police procedural that follows the thin trail of the victim's clues that eventually lead to the witness, the murderer, a potential romance and a satisfying conclusion. Stratton was a prolific crime fiction writer during this era. He also wrote at least one story under the name Terry Spain.

Hot Eyes
by Dean Evans ★★★

A businessman, blinded on principle, can't see the monumental abuse his wife heaps upon him until his loyal secretary bursts his illusions. His new found knowledge triggers an ability to spontaneously ignite the sources of his anger. Dean Evans was one of several pseudonyms used by Robert Arthur (of *Mysterious Traveler* and *Three Investigators* fame), and this yarn certainly seems to fit his MO.

You Killed Elizabeth
by Brett Halliday ★★★★★

The loyalty of two best friends is tested when the perfect woman comes between them. Halliday builds tension masterfully as romance blooms and the killer of the title is finally revealed.

Give Back the Dead
by James Robbins Miller ★★★

Inspired ". . . by a woman receiving a letter from a friend who had died a week before, in which he told of future plans." Miller transforms the concept into an upscale melodrama good enough for *Collier's*, where it first ran in 1949 as "Letters from Cairo."

Murder Town
by Raymond Drennen ★★★★

Drennen's pulp fiction career spanned a neat ten years: 1947–1957. It began with Street and Smith's *Detective Story Magazine* and ended with *Terror Detective Story Magazine*. "Himself a man of action, he's shoved thousands of fellahin [Egyptian laborers] up and down the Nile, wrangled with Nazi agents in Cairo and worked on a hydrogen bomb project for the A.E.C. [Atomic Energy Commission], in North Carolina."

His novelette opens with "A rain of blood, a prevalence of corpses, and a deadly puzzle for Jim Brady made the sinful city of Jordanville into a . . . Murder Town."

Jim Brady, private operative,

catches wind of trouble in Jordanville on a routine background check for a client. He's soon swallowed up in a racket that involves mobsters, crooked cops, a Treasury Agent, slot machines and opium. Drennen is a fine writer. His story is a fast paced, carefully plotted, action-packed mini-saga reminiscent of "Red Harvest." My only quibble is the hero is so perfect, he pushes the boundaries of suspended disbelieve. The unlikely female Treasury Agent, Gloria Yale, sums it up, "Bill Shumate said you were good, Jim. Now I've been here six months, and it took you twenty-four hours to start from scratch and break it open."

Drennen wrote at least two crime novels, *You'll Die Now* (1953) and *Murder Beat* (1956). He died in 1967 in Philadelphia, at the age of 67.

The final story of the *Suspense* digests is a "storyette," a filler for the final page. With only a single page to work with McLaughlin does a fine job setting up a desperate situation, planning its aftermath and taking the fatal last step from which there is no return.

Michael L. Cook wrote in *Mystery, Detective, and Espionage Magazines*, "If the fourth issue was all that good [akin to a more pulp-oriented issue of *EQMM*], why was it the final one? The two-color covers and the fact that the first three issues, best stories by the big-name, buyer-getting authors, are nearly all reprints suggests an all-too-familiar answer: inadequate financing. The money may have run out just as the 1950's *Suspense* was on the verge of success. If only the fourth issue could have been the first."

The Way Out
by Lorrie McLaughlin ★★★★

One might think this magazine is called *Suspense Stories*, but it's actually a one-shot entitled *9 of the World's Most Exciting Suspense Stories*, published by Consolidated Book Publishers in 1945. Compiled by R.M. Barrows, it includes stories by Richard Connell, Wilkie Collins, Damon Runyon (two), Richard Middleton, Agatha Christie, John G. Craig, Frederic J. Stimson, and Robert Louis Stevenson. Remarkably, it includes at least one illustration on every spread throughout its 96 pages, by J. Allen St. John, Stan Lilstrom, Martin Garrity, Robert Sinnott, Bob Logan and Milt Youngren. At 6" x 9," it originally sold for 13¢. Note the Best Books logo on its cover, which was painted by Stan Lilstrom. It was part of a short-lived series that included *11 of the World's Great War & Spy Stories* and *12 of the World's Great Humor Stories*, both published in 1944.

Suspense Magazine
Contents and Reprint Sources

Suspense Magazine #1 Spring 1951
Science Fiction
"The Deathless Ones" by John Chapman and Oliver Saari
"Obviously Suicide" by S. Fowler Wright
"The Quick and the Bomb" by William Tenn

Mystery
"A Most Amazing Murder" by A.B. Shiffrin
"Honeymoon Terror" by John Dickson Carr originally titled "Cabin B-13" *EQMM* May 1944, dramatized for radio on *Suspense* March 16, 1943

Crime
"The Eyewitness Who Wouldn't See" by James A. Kitch originally titled "Murder for Two" from *Argosy* June 1949

Fantasy
"Jeannie and the Light Brown Cure" by Alexander Samalman originally titled "Medical Note" from *Thrilling Wonder Stories* Feb. 1942
"Ghost of a Chance" by Theodore Sturgeon originally titled "The Green-Eyed Monster" *Unknown Worlds* June 1943

The Macabre
"Voice in the Night" by William Hope Hodgson reprinted from *The Blue Book Magazine* Nov. 1907
"Small Assassin" by Ray Bradbury reprinted from *Dime Mystery Magazine* Nov. 1946

Suspense Storyette
"She Didn't Bounce" by Peter Phillips

Detective Novelette
"Faces Turned Against Him" by John Gearon

Suspense Magazine #2 Summer 1951
Science Fiction
"Operation Peep" by John Wyndham
"World Within" by Thomas A. Coffee

Mystery
"Blood Will Tell" by Nathaniel Weyl
"The Nightmare Face" by Walter Snow
"Elusive Witness" by Georges Simenon

Adventure
"Survival" by Thomas Gilchrist

Crime
"Fatal Mistake" by John Basye Price
"Criminal at Large" by Larry Holden
"Pardon My Terror" by Irving Burstiner
"Evil Is the Night" by Edith Saylor Abbot

The Macabre
"Black Death" by John Krill
"Maiden Beware" by Richard Lewis first broadcast on *Suspense* July 1944 as "The Black Shawl"
"A Horseman in the Sky" by Ambrose Bierce reprinted from *San Francisco Examiner* April 14, 1889

Fantasy
"Penny Wise, Fate Foolish" by Mary Elizabeth Counselman retitled from "The Three Marked Pennies" from *Weird Tales* Aug. 1934

Novelette
"The Perfectly Calm Murder" by F. Hugh Herbert

Suspense Magazine #3 Fall 1951
Mystery
"Not a Leg to Stand On" by Don Mardick
"You Can't Run Away" by Philip Weck

Science Adventure
"Dear Automaton" by A. E. van Vogt retitled from "Automaton" from *Other Worlds Science Stories* Sep. 1950

Dread Dilemma
"The Saboteur" by William Sambrot
"Wall of Fear" by Will F. Jenkins retitled from "No More Walls"

from *Collier's* June 26, 1937
"The Seventh Man" by Sir Arthur T. Quiller-Couch from *Old Fires and Profitable Ghosts*, Scribner's 1900

The Fantastic
"Love Ethereal" by Horace L. Gold
"How Can You Be Reading This?" by Charles H. Gesner

The Macabre
"The Thing on the Snow" by Waldo Carlton Wright

Criminals At Large
"My Favorite Corpse" by Dorothy F. Horton
"Rip Tide" by Russell Branch
"Terror in the Sun" by Talmage Powell ("Talmadge" on the cover)
"Pattern for Dying" by Morris Cooper

Novelette
"Dark Vengeance" by Fritz Leiber, Jr.

Suspense Magazine #4 Winter 1952
Deadly Danger
"Threat of Violence" by R. J. Burrough

Mystery
"And Never Came Back" by Dorothy Marie Davis

"You Killed Elizabeth" by Brett Halliday also appeared in the *The London Mystery Magazine* #8, Feb/Mar 1951

Chiller-Thriller
"The Screaming Woman" by Ray Bradbury reprint from *Today, The* [Philadelphia] *Inquirer Magazine* May 27, 1951

Dread Dilemma
"Ask No Quarter" by Duane Yarnell
"Give Back the Dead" by James Robbins Miller reprint of "Letters from Cairo" *Collier's* June 11, 1949
"The Way Out" by Lorrie McLaughlin

Fantasy
"Hot Eyes" by Dean Evans

Crime Corner
"The Third Degree" by Charles Lenart
"Find the Witness" by Ted Stratton

Novelette
"Murder Town" by Raymond Drennen

Note: Stories and categories are listed in the order they appear on the Contents page of each issue. The story snopyses are listed in the order they appear in the issues.

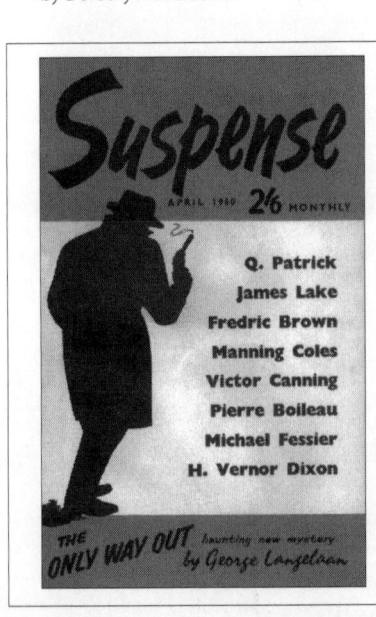

The British *Suspense* digest magazine from Fleetway Publications, had no relation to the CBS property, but it was far more successful in terms of longevity. The monthly magazine made its debut in August 1958 and ran for 32 issues until April 1961. In May 1961 it was incorporated into the British *Argosy* magazine, which also had no relation to the US magazine of that title. *Suspense* began with a 160-page count but settled in at 144 pages before too long. It included some reprints but also offered many original stories. Its authors included Agatha Christie, Dashiell Hammett, John Dickson Carr, Leslie Charteris, James Lake, Georges Simenon, Ray Bradbury, Edgar Wallace, Thomas Walsh, George Langelaan, John Masters, Victor Canning, Hugh Pentecost, Christianna Brand and dozens of others.

Suspense Novels
Article by Richard Krauss

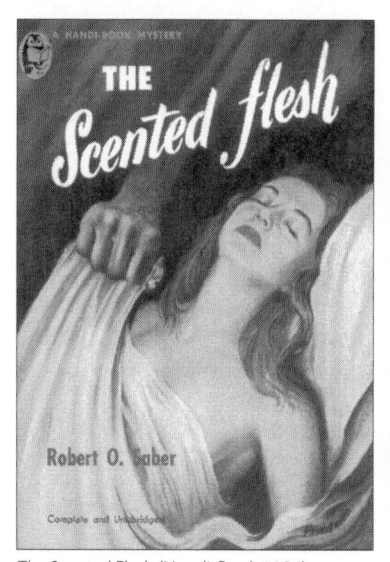

The Scented Flesh (Handi-Book #124) cover by Mike Privitello

Madman on a Drum (Ramble House edition with Calvalcade Books cover art)

A half-page ad in *Suspense Magazine* #4 offered a series of three Suspense Novels, companion digest/paperbacks to the anthology title, all published in 1951. The offer combined all three, along with a copy of *The Scented Flesh* by Robert O. Saber, also in the digest/paperback format, for a buck, postage paid. (Robert O. Saber was a pseudonym of Milton K. Ozaki, who wrote over 20 crime novels. *The Scented Flesh* was one of his earlier efforts, published as Handi-Book #124.)

Madman on a Drum written by *Suspense* contributing editor N.R. De Mexico, was first published in 1944 by Cavalcade Books based in New York, as a digest-sized paperback. In 1951 it was retitled *Strange Pursuit* and featured as the first of three Suspense Novels from Farrell Publishing.

Also in 1951, De Mexico's *Marijuana Girl* was published, drawing notoriety in 1952 as a prime example of "artful appeals to sensuality, immorality, filth, perversion and degeneracy" by the U.S. House of Representatives' Select Committee on Current Pornographic Materials, aka the Gathings Committee.

The notoriety didn't deter de Mexico's *Private Chauffeur*, published in 1952 as Intimate Novel #15. For years the identity of De Mexico was under speculation until Fender Tucker sleuthed him out as Robert Bragg, and reported in Gary Lovisi's *Paperback Parade* #69: "According to his son, Kim, 'the pen name N.R. De Mexico means 'N' for nee (born), 'R' for Robert of Mexico. I think the Mexico was a gag because at one point he had taught himself to speak Spanish well enough for him to translate for some additional income. During the war he worked for military intelligence. In the years just after WWII he was an editor for an architectural magazine, and only began writing novels after that period.'"

Strange Pursuit (*Madman on a Drum*) is a top notch thriller, cleverly plotted with beautifully written narrative and dialogue. When Lois Vincent fails to keep a date with boyfriend Larry Graham, the mystery of her disappearance sparks a surreal, paranoid crisis for Graham that quickly escalates into a full-blown conspiracy in which he can trust no one as he doggedly fights to clear himself of her murder and figure out who could so completely destroy his life.

De Mexico uses second person narrative in several sections to emphasize the panic and disorientation of his protagonist. Here's an example:

"He began to run back toward the Square. Then he stopped. Dead. He hadn't really heard it, had he? That was just his imagination playing tricks on him.

"You didn't hear your name called out in public like that—not unless it was a contest you had entered, or some other silly thing.

"But he had heard it. The sound of her voice was clear and precise and detailed—tonal and vital, violently inflected and genuine."

De Mexico also clearly enjoys writing out sound effects. Here's a couple of bits of his magic:

"He stepped through into the bedlam of typewriters, adding machines, comptometers, automatic billing machines. (Clickety, smackety, blickety, pop. Bungety, clango, clinkety, plop.)"

And:

"Funny word. Murder. Roll it over on your tongue. Taste it. Feel its caustic bitterness. Murder. Herder, girder. Only two other words like it in the whole language. And murderer! There was no herderer and no girderer. No other triple-er word in the language."

Ramble House has collected all three of De Mexico's novels in a print and ebook anthology The N.R. De Mexico Novels (*Private Chauffeur*, *Marijuana Girl* and *Madman on a Drum*).

The second Suspense Novel was an original, *The Case of the Lonely Lovers* by Will Daemer, published in 1951. A pseudonym, Will Daemer, is an anagram for Wade Miller, the writing team of Robert Wade and Bill Miller, who also wrote as Dale Wilmer (another anagram) and more famously as

Suspense Novel #1 *Strange Pursuit* by N.R. de Mexico

Whit Masterson and Wade Miller.

Perhaps their most famous novel as Whit Masterson, *Badge of Evil* (1956), was the source of Orson Welles' screenplay for his film noir classic *Touch of Evil* (1958).

The Wade/Miller team wrote over thirty novels together. Their lifelong friendship began in childhood; they attended San Diego State together and even enlisted in the US Air Force in unison. Both writers were born in 1920. Bill Miller died much earlier, in 1961, while Robert Wade lived to the age of 92, until his death in 2012.

After 1961, Wade continued his writing career as a solo novelist and a movie and television scriptwriter. He was honored with several awards over his career, including the Private Eye Writers of America's Lifetime Achievement Award in 1988.

The Case of the Lonely Lovers opens with a dark-eyed, young woman, one Betty Ackerman, dressed in a gayly flowered frock, running for her life. She chances upon an isolated house, its reluctant owner, Robert Muir, and his massive dog, Kahn. Only the mystery of what and why loomed larger than the danger and desperation hinged on her disagreeable host, reluctant to help a damsel so obviously in need.

She explains she was kidnapped and how she only escaped by a stroke of luck. She pleads for him to believe her, to which he replies, "It doesn't make any difference whether I believe you or not."

A knock interrupts their strained conversation. A voice through the door, a police detective yells, "We're looking for an escaped prisoner by the name of Betty Ackerman . . . I'd like to take a look around."

But the ornery churl shares his aversion to the needs of others freely. He denies the detective entry, seeing it as the shortest route to end further interruption and investigation. Betty is quick to capitalize, and ekes out permission to stay the night, as he grudgingly unlocks one of the upstairs bedrooms for her.

Ed Lynskey, on MysteryFile.com, quotes the back cover copy from *Evil Come, Evil Go*, about Wade and Miller's writing process.

In part: "After discussing an idea at length, they outline extensively." For me, this technique shows prominently in the tight plotting of *The Case of the Lonely Lovers*.

Tension builds masterfully as the fog of mystery behind "The Case" slowly clears. A conspiracy, with Betty unknowingly thrust into its center, in the fight of her life.

And while the main plot heats up, Wade and Miller simultaneously fuel the romantic triangle of Betty, her boyfriend Glen Proctor, and Muir, as she steadily thaws the cold heart of her reluctant host.

Most of the prose is purposefully composed, driving the plot, character depth or the emotional impact of the action. But a few lines stand out as more poetic, like this one near the climax: "She blamed the thin fog that had been sucked inland by yesterday's heat and drifted like a grey broth at the windows."

Like the first Suspense Novel, *The Case of the Lonely Lovers* is a terrific read, one that seems perfectly ripe for a new printing. Which could be said with equal conviction for the third and final novel of the series.

Carl G. Hodges (1902–1964) was born in Quincy, Illinois. He worked for the National Association of Petroleum Retailers, the Illinois Department of Public Welfare and the state's Information Service; and as a journalist for the *Peoria Star*. He was also a prolific fiction writer whose stories appeared in *Mystery Magazine*, *Thrilling Detective*, *Famous Detective Stories*, *Crime Story Magazine*, *Manhunt* and *Calling All Boys*; and even a two-page prose story for *Air Fighters Comics* in 1941. He wrote novelettes for Hearst

Suspense Novel #2 *The Case of the Lonely Lovers* by Will Daemer

Features and contributed articles to house organs and travel journals.

Of his seven novels, four were intended for young readers: *Baxie Randall and the Blue Raiders* (1962), *Dobie Sturis and the Dog Soldiers* (1963), *Benjie Ream* (1964) and *Land Rush* (1965). This final novel, *Land Rush*, was published a year after his death, and awarded the Western Heritage Award in 1966. *Benjie Ream* was selected for "The Black Experience in Children's Books" collection by the New

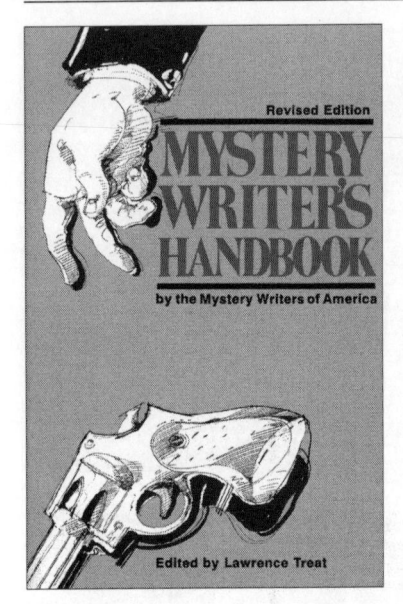

York Public Library in 1971.

His three crime novels were published a decade earlier: *Naked Villainy* (1951), *Crime on My Hands* (1952), and *Murder By the Pack* (1953), half of an Ace Double with *About Face* by Frank Kane.

Hodges helped organize and lead the Springfield Civil War Round Table, where he served as president. He also served as vice-president of the Midwest chapter of the Mystery Writers of America (MWA), which may have been his connection to the Chicago office of Farrell Publishing.

Farrell published *Naked Villainy* as the third and final "Original Suspense Novel" in 1951. It's a carefully plotted mystery with hardboiled characters whose voices define their attitudes in Hodges' entertaining prose. As the opening clearly demonstrates:

"Rain swam down the pane on the back door as I rapped with my knuckles. I bent over and peered through the V of the divided chintz curtains. I saw a lamp glowing on a table but there was no sound inside the apartment so I used my knuckles again. For good measure I banged my Florsheim against the the lower panel."

Back then, you might find a novel's cast list upfront. That's the case here on the inside front cover. It's a preview, but also useful reference if you find yourself needing reorientation between reading sessions. Wick Davis is one of Chicago's finest, with a weakness for the ladies. His brother Clark's pursuit of law enforcement went elsewhere, as an insurance investigator. It's a little complicated, but they both knew stripteaser Inez Fischetti, before she was murdered. Wick needs to find out who did it, preferably before somebody else joins her. That doesn't work out so well, but eventually he's got enough clues to piece together the truth for the final showdown.

Of all the digests in Farrell's series, *Naked Villainy* is the most provocative. The story's first victim is shown on the cover in a sheer bra and panties—exactly what she's wearing in the opening chapter.

"The light was weak, but good enough so that the black panties held no mystery."

And later: "She had whirled to face me, one hand jerking up from the front of the black bra and tearing the flimsy cloth. A nipple pointed at me, the color of a pecan on top of a cup cake." Steamy prose for 1951.

Hodges' reverence for the Midwest MWA provides a wonderful surprise mid-novel, when Lieutenant Davis visits one of the chapter's meetings. Chapter president Bill Brannon is on hand, a journalist and crime fiction writer with report-

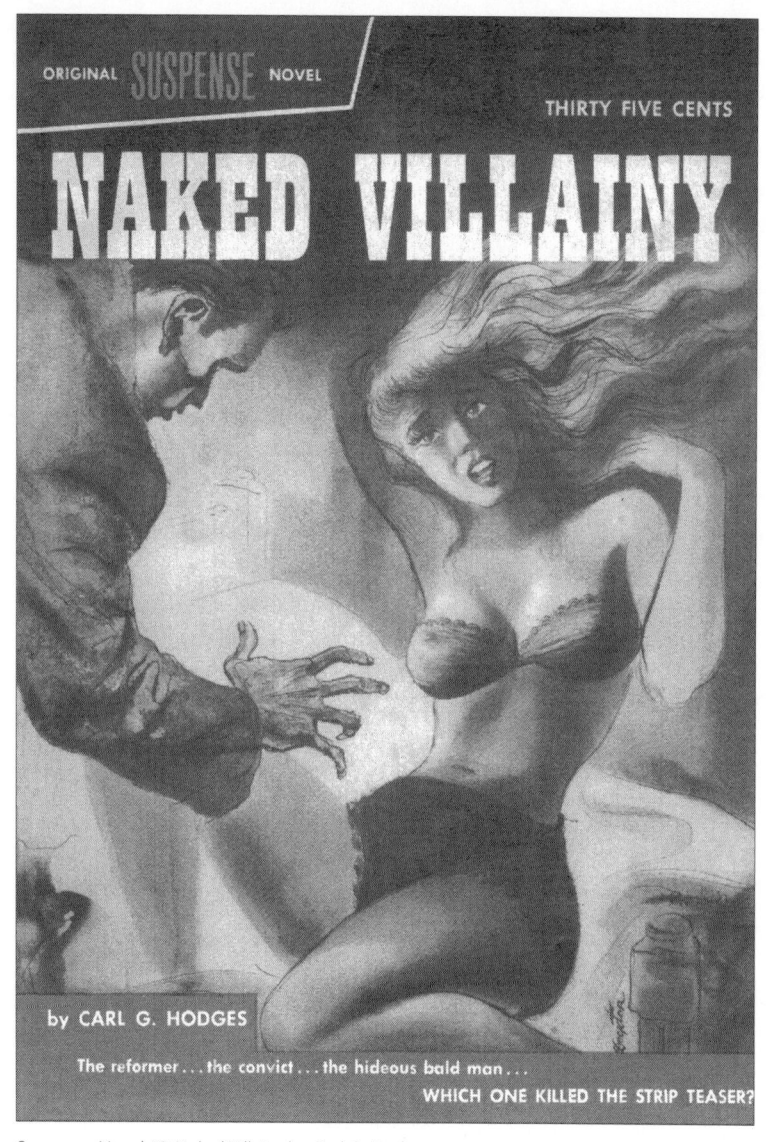

Suspense Novel #3 *Naked Villainy* by Carl G. Hodges

edly over 5,000 stories and articles to his credit. His biography of con man Joseph Weil, *Yellow Kid Weil*, is mentioned, but Brannon wrote several other books as well as stories for *Coronet, Reader's Digest, Omnibook, Saga, Ellery Queen's Mystery Magazine* and many others. He used his middle name Tibbetts, to write as William Tibbetts, one of more than a half-dozen pseudonyms he used. Known as "The Dean of Crime Writers," Brannon was nominated for the Edgar Award in 1951.

In 1976, MWA produced the *Mystery Writer's Handbook*, under the guidance of Lawrence Treat. Each chapter tackles an element of the craft, written by a veritable who's who of the industry. William T. Brannon is onboard with a chapter on how to write true crime. According to Treat: "After reading it, all you need is to go out and do it."

Back at the fictitious MWA meeting, Lennie Hilts had just sold *From Jennys to Jets*. As it turned out the book was published in 1951, as *The Airmail Jennies to Jets* as told to Leonard Finley Hilts.

Milton Ozaki, who apparently coiffed hair by day, and had a "police dog" named Sacre Bleu, receives a quarter page tribute. His novels, *A Fiend in Need*, *The Cuckoo Clock* and *Too Many Women* are mentioned—as is his pseudonym, Robert O. Saber.

Another MWA member, Allen Pruitt, identified by his pseudonym "because he was Commissioner of Public Welfare of the City of Chicago and I guess he figured it would be better to use a pen name for his excursions into the mystery writing field." This was actually Alvin Emanuel Rose, a Chicago journalist in the 1920s and 1930s prior to becoming Commissioner. He wrote two novels as Alan Pruitt, *The Restless Corpse* (1947), which Hodges mentions, and *Typed For a Corpse*, in 1954.

The final attendee was Paul Fairman, author of *The Glass Ladder*, Harlequin #139. Fairman's work appeared most often in *Ellery Queen's Mystery Magazine*, but he also sold to *The Saint*, *Alfred Hitchcock's Mystery Magazine*, *Mike Shayne*, *Shell Scott*—and earlier in pulps like *Black Mask*, *FBI Detective Stories* and *Mammoth Detective*. He also wrote as Paul Daniels.

Getting back to Hodges, *Naked Villainy*, is an excellent digest original that can easily leave you searching for more of his work. One of his short stories, "Murder Throws a Ringer" from *Thrilling Detective* (Dec. 1947), is included in *The Noir Mystery Megapack* from Wildside Press.

Bulldog Drummond by Sapper
Review by Richard Krauss

"Enormous physical strength is a great asset, but it carries with it certain natural disadvantages. In the first place, its possessor is frequently clumsy: Hugh had practised in France till he could move over ground without a single blade of grass rustling."

Early in the 20th century it was not permitted for officers serving the British Army to publish under their proper names. Thus, Herman Cyril McNeile was given the pen name "Sapper" by the owner of the *Daily Mail*, Lord Northcliffe.

Sapper's Bulldog Drummond began as a policeman in his first appearance in a short story published in *The Strand Magazine*, but McNeile transformed the character into a gentleman adventurer for the first novel, published in 1920.

The language used in the book reflects its era, nationality and commonly accepted prejudices, which call attention to themselves at least once every few pages. A humorous example; as Drummond and his pals recover from being drugged the Captain quips, "However, while you go and put your nuts in the river, I'll go up and make certain."

In this case "nuts" means "heads."

Another convention of the times, is the inclusion of the chapter number in its title: "Chapter one in which he takes tea at the Carlton and is surprised."

The British edition shown here is Hodder and Stoughton's soft cover from 1953. The first of 19 in the series, ten of which were penned by McNeile and continued by his friend Gerard Fairlie after McNeile's death in 1937. It might be considered a paperback, but its dimensions and overall feel align with Fleetway's *Suspense* magazine, so I will treat it as the first of a digest series.

The quality production values and heavy-weight cover stock of this 1953 edition, made the volume easier to hold and handle than a typical 60-year-old digest. If only more publishers had followed suit.

As the story opens it's Decem-

ber 1918, just a month after the end of the first great war, at the Hotel National in Berne. Count Comte de Guy gathers a trio of wealthy businessmen, Mr. Hocking, an American, and two Germans, Herr Steinemann and Herr von Gratz, to finance his scheme to mount the defeat of England. "... a defeat more utter and complete than if she had lost the war...." (WWI) They agree on the condition that de Guy convince another wealthy American, Hiram Potts, to join them and reduce each man's investment to a quarter, rather than a third of the total required.

Meanwhile, Captain Hugh Drummond, late of the Royal Loamshires, reviews responses to his blind box newspaper ad seeking adventure. From the stack of letters, one catches his eye and leads to a meeting with Phyllis Benton, and coincidentally Henry Lakington, whom she later confides is "the second most dangerous man in England."

Of course this begs the question, who is number one? A man named Carl Peterson, whom Lakington reports to. It seems Phyllis' father has somehow been unwillingly drawn into a conspiracy hatched by Peterson, and Miss Benton hopes Drummond is just the man to set things right.

Like most classic pulp heroes Drummond is wealthy, extraordinarily fit, remarkably adept at numerous fighting skills, a born leader and irresistible. (In Drummond's case "his best friend would not have called him good-looking," but his smile is devastating. "He smiled, and no woman yet born could see Hugh Drummond smile without smiling too.")

His archetype is always freed from conventional problems and concerns, apparently so all of their energies can be focused on their altruistic missions—none of the normal baggage and responsibilities of life to weight them down.

Unfortunately, all this damned perfection can also make them boring. Sapper was a fine writer, but his efforts to continuously ensure readers understand the remarkable character and humility of his hero is at times tedious.

At the other extreme, Drummond is transformed to near absurdity in the presence of the love of his life, Miss Benton. His normal heroic ability is reduced to the level of an awkward teenager when they're alone on the page.

My first encounter with Bulldog Drummond, from the old time radio program, was very favorable. I was preconditioned to enjoy this novel, and if I'd read it alongside the exploits of David Innes and Curt Newman, back in high school, I may well have loved every minute of it. But coming at it fresh, nearly a century after it was written, I found it difficult to enjoy.

After an excellent prologue sets up the impending crisis, the meandering plot takes a hundred pages or more to bring the threat back into the story's primary focus. There are moments of excitement—paralyzing gas, a gorilla at large and an insidious chemical bath, to mention a few—but nearly every scene is mired in verbose narrative that sucks the momentum and urgency from the action.

Bulldog Drummond was a bestselling series for thirty years. The first novel was adapted for stage, where it ran for 428 performances. Popular radio and movie series were based on the hero's exploits. The character inspired Ian Fleming's James Bond. Drummond's place in the halls of adventure fiction fame is unequivocal.

It would be ridiculous to deny the quality of the prose or the popularity of the character. It's a classic. Just be aware it's firmly rooted in the style and sensibilities of its era, which for me overshadowed its many merits.

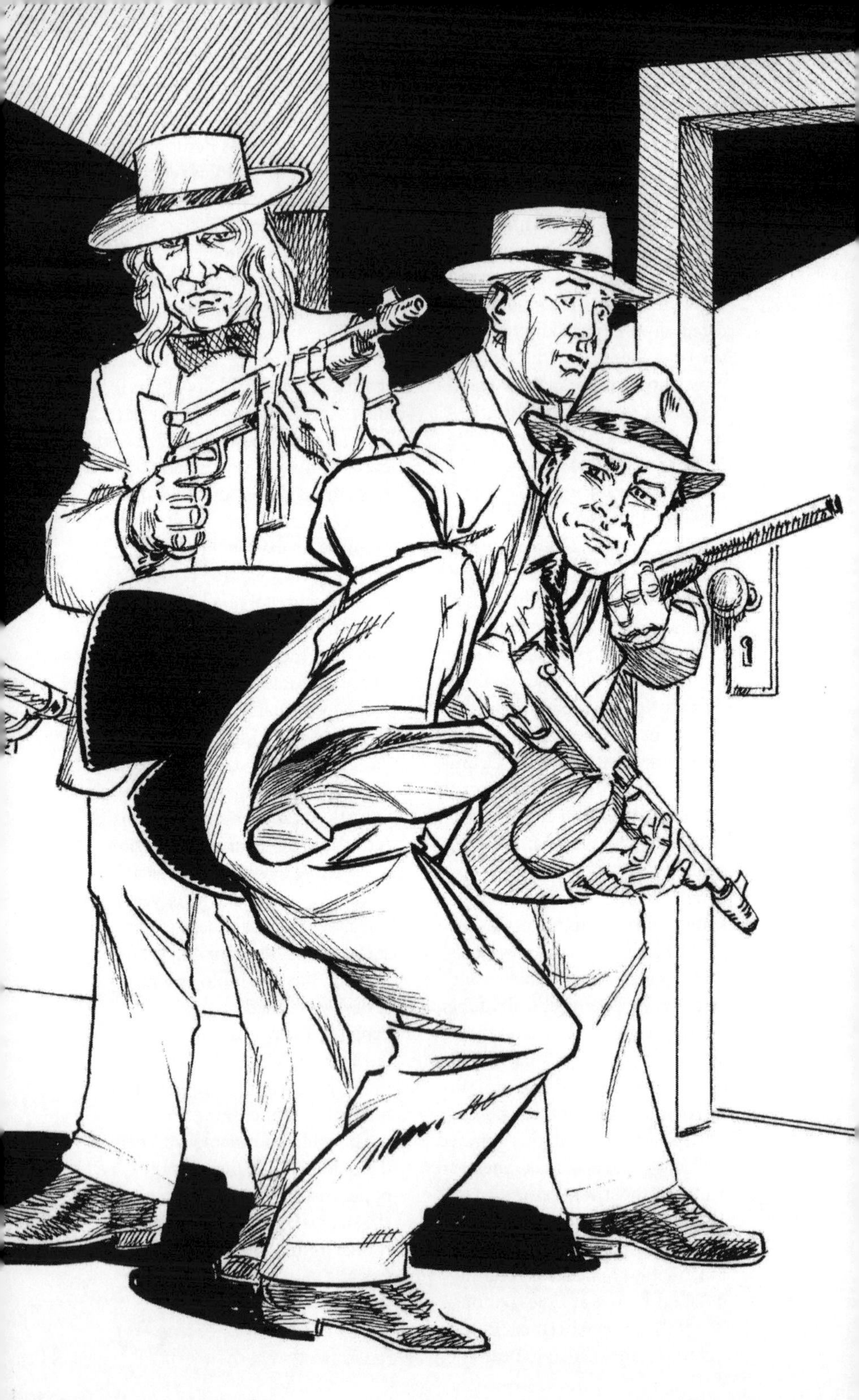

The Hideout

A Brother Bones story by Ron Fortier
Illustrations by Rob Davis

"Bones, you are needed." Within the shimmering yellow flame he saw the tiny angelic face of his spirit guide; a teenage girl he'd shot to death in his previous life as gunman Tommy Bonello.

It was long after midnight and most of the patrons in Old Town's Gridiron saloon had long since packed it up and gone home; wherever in Cape Noire was home to each of them. Of course there were always the night owls who hung around till whenever owner Butch Hammer decided to lock up.

On this particular muggy summer night, three of Hammer's regulars were seated around one of the dozen round tables that filled the small bar. Similarly dressed in worn, dark suits and fedoras, the three sat drinking bottle after bottle of Wyld Ale, the new beer recently bought from Alexis Wyld's new brewery acquisition on the outskirts of the city. Not that any of the trio were connoisseurs, they had decided on the new drink because it was being sold cheaper than most of the other labels in town. It was a promotional gimmick and by the number of empty soldiers scattered amongst the butt-filled ashtrays on the table's surface, was a mild success.

"Fifty thousands dollars to anyone who brings her the head of Brother Bones!" Michael Brown said and then made a fist, hit his chest and burped. "Can you believe that? Fifty thousand smackers for taking out one guy!"

"He ain't just one guy," corrected Mark Kalita who sat to Brown's right. "You know damn well Brother Bones is some kind of spook. She's been trying to bump him off for a couple of years now and come up snake-eyes every time." He grabbed his bottle and drained it in one swallow.

"How do you even know that's true?" asked the youngest of the three, long haired Gerald Kuster. "I mean, why the hell would a dame like Alexis Wyld put a bounty on a character like Bones? Don't make no sense at all." He lifted his hat and scratched his hair. His dandruff always made his scalp itch.

"What?" Brown, the older of the three snapped. "Where da hell you been hiding these past three years, Gerald?" No one called Kuster, Jerry. He hated that nickname. "It was Brother Bones who murdered her father, you know . . . the old crime boss of Cape Noire, Topper Wyld."

"Ah, I thought that was just a bullshit story some of the guys made up."

"Well, it ain't, pal." Brown twisted in his chair and held up one of the empties. "Hey, Butch, how about another round."

The bartender/owner nodded and went to the cooler as Kuster continued their discussion. "So where'd you hear she'd put out a bounty on him?"

"Ran into one of her top guns, Reed Vengel."

"You mean that rat-faced little guy who likes to use knives instead guns?" Kuster, like most of the criminal element in the port city, was all too familiar with the hood in question.

"The one and the same, Gerald," Brown concluded. "Ran into him while getting a haircut downtown. He and his crew are spreading the word all over town. Miss Wylde wants Bones' head on a platter and is willing to shell out fifty thousand gees to make it happen."

"Shit," Kuster nodded, dropping his fedora on the empty chair beside him. "That's a lot of freaking money."

"Agreed," Kalita chimed in. With straight black hair, he was the charmer of the group; a real lady's man. Fishing into his fancy suit jacket, he pulled out a pack of smokes and lit one up with his Zippo. "But you know what bugs the shit out of me, guys?"

"Nah," the older Brown played along. "What has your shorts in a twist, pally?"

"Simply this," Kalita blew out a puff of gray smoke. "For almost three years this skull-faced wacko has been running around all over this damn town putting the bloody fear of God in our criminal fellowship. And not only has he gotten away with it, but no one still has a goddamn clue as to who he really is—or where the hell his hideout's at! Now does that make any sense to you guys?" Kalita slammed an open hand on the table rattling the empty bottles.

"Well, gee," Kuster said. "Maybe his hideout is in that airship thingee he's always flying around in."

Kalita looked at his friend and tried to make sense of his statement. "Huh? What the hell are you talking about now, kid?"

"You know . . . the bone-ship or some such . . . that they talk about on his radio show every week."

Kalita couldn't believe his ears. Brown started laughing.

"What?" Kuster was confused. "You guys never heard his radio show?"

"God save me," Brown managed to get out between loud chuckles. "He thinks the freaking radio show is for real!"

Kuster looked at Brown with a hurt expression. "Huh?"

"Jezzuz, you moron," Kalita couldn't help himself. "And I suppose you think the Lone Ranger and Captain Midnight are real too?"

For a second, Kuster looked like he was about to either cry or get up and hit somebody. Before he could choose either reaction, Butch arrived with three fresh brews on a tray. He set it down, removed the bottles; passing one to each of his customers and then began setting the empties on it.

"Couldn't help overhearing your conversation," Hammer said, his mouth wrapped around a half-smoked, foul smelling cigar. "You wanta know where that Brother Bones is hiding out, you oughta ask Old Gus over there in the corner."

Brown, Kalita and Kuster all swiveled about in their chairs to look at the old man slumped over the table in the far back corner. Old Gus Reinerman was an established fixture in the Gridiron. During his youth he'd been a seaman who, according to his tall tales, had sailed around the world a dozen times. When he lost his leg to a great white shark off the Philippines, he'd come home to Cape Noire to settle down. Hammer hired him as a janitor and let him sleep in the storage room located in the back of the bar.

"You're kidding, right?" Kalita asked scrutinizing the barkeep to see if he was joking with them.

"Nope. You know how Old Gus rants and raves all the time and spins his stories to get a free drink from the regulars. Well, a few nights ago while he was cleaning up the place, he told me he'd seen that Brother Bones guy come out of some nice brownstone somewhere here in the city."

Hammer picked up the now full tray balancing it with one hand and started to go back to the bar. "I didn't pay it no mind, but hearing you guys talk about that reward and all got me remembering it."

"You think he was telling the truth?" Brown asked Hammer's back.

"How the hell would I know," the big Irishman said over his shoulder. "Talk to him or not. It's no skin off my nose."

Brown looked at his mates. Neither said a word but eyed each other in silence. "Aw hell," he finally uttered grabbing his new beer. "What we got to lose?"

He pushed back from the table and got off his chair; Kalita and Kuster did the same. Together they sauntered over to the table in the back shadows.

"Hey, Gus," Brown called loudly. "Wake up, we wanta talk to you."

An hour later a fancy black sedan pulled up to the curb in the middle of a nice, well kept block. Streetlamps gave off a soft glow painting the brownstones and other apartment buildings a muted gray color. The expensive car, less than two months old, belonged to Michael Brown and he loved driving it. The few other parked sedans in this neighborhood were mostly rundown, second hand vehicles. As this was a blue-collar part of town, they were all the locals could afford.

"You sure this is the right place?" Mark Kalita inquired from the front passenger seat. He was looking up at the six-story tenement building they had parked in front of.

"That's the number Old Gus said," Brown shut off the headlights and killed the engine. "The place he saw Brother Bones go into."

The old sailor, once they had shaken him awake, had related the story of how months earlier, while on a drinking toot with several of his old sea mates, he'd gotten lost and wandered through this part of town drunk as a skunk. He'd collapsed on the stoop of the building across the street, nursing a bottle of rum and then fallen asleep. Later that night he'd been awaken by the sound of a car pulling up in front of this very building and from it had emerged the Undead Avenger accompanied by a young man. Old Gus had seen them go into the building and a few seconds later spied the lights flash up on the third floor. After they were extinguished, he had passed out again.

Come the next morning he'd walked to the nearest bus stop and caught a ride back to Old Town and the Gridiron. It wasn't until weeks later when he'd seen a sketch of Brother Bones in the newspaper that he had remembered both the incident and, more importantly, the address of the place itself. He had told this to Hammer and some of the other Gridiron crew but all of them just ignored his claim as just another of his alcoholic induced fabrications.

Until now.

"I don't see no roadster," Kalita pointed out as he opened the door and exited.

Getting out of his own door, Brown looked up and down the street. Of the three autos on it, none was a roadster. "Hell, that don't mean nothing. Could be parked out in a back alley somewhere. If there's a chance this Bones spook is living here, then I'm gonna find out and then we can talk how we're gonna split that fifty gees."

At the same time Gerald Kuster had come out of the back seat and gone around to the rear to pull open the trunk. Brown came over to flank his left side while Kalita his right. The trio looked down at the weapons stored there; two Thompson submachine guns and one double-barrel shotgun. Brown and Kalita hoisted the machine guns while Kuster hefted the big shotgun and then quietly lowered the trunk lid. As the three moved away from the sedan, Kuster broke open the shotgun. He took two shells from his jacket pocket and slid them into the twin breaches before closing the chamber again.

Brown led the way up the concrete stairs and jerked back one of the two doors and entered the small vestibule. Kalita caught the open door and followed him inside. Kuster held the door wide with the tip of his weapon and gave the deserted street a final look before doing the same.

Minutes later they were climbing the hallway's stairs.

In the coldwater flat, the man who doesn't sleep sat in his chair looking out the window at Cape Noire. His black, lifeless eyes never stopped gazing out at the tall, high rise towers beyond the bucolic park only a few blocks away. Because he didn't sleep he also did not dream, but rather was himself the living embodiment of a nightmare.

He was Brother Bones, the Undead Avenger and he simply sat and waited.

He waited for the candle on the bureau behind him to flicker with light which meant he was needed to bring vengeance to those who spread evil throughout his city.

And just as it had done so many times before, the tiny white hot flame miraculously appeared, surrounding the pitch black tiny wick. Light glowed in the small, square room and Bones turned his head at the flame's appearance. He silently got up from his chair and walked to the bureau where the candle was set. Next to it was a porcelain white mask. He stood and gazed deep into the heart of the fire.

"*Bones, you are needed.*" Within the shimmering yellow flame he saw the tiny angelic face of his spirit guide; a teenage girl he'd shot to death in his previous life as gunman Tommy Bonello. Now she served the mysterious fates as their conduit to him in this zombie-like incarnation. He was not allowed the eternal rest of death until his mission for them had been fulfilled.

"What?" His was voice was deep, cold and without feeling.

"*Three men are coming for you. They seek your demise at the bidding of Alexis Wylde.*"

The thing that was Brother Bones showed no reaction to the name of his enemy. He had too many to bother worrying about any of them individually—if, in fact, he was capable of worry. How does one worry a dead man?

"I will deal with them."

The lovely young face seem to smile whimsically and then faded away.

Brother Bones opened the bureau's top drawer where he kept

his twin .45 silver plated automatics in their leather rig. He slipped it over his shoulders and made sure both were snug under his arms. Then he picked up the mask and placed it over the horror that was the remains of his one time handsome face. Rotted with decay, it had the power to make men go mad should they ever look upon it.

The candle flame winked out. Bones grabbed his topcoat and floppy slouch hat from the coat rack and then walked out of his room. He glided through the darkened kitchen in the apartment he shared with card dealer, Blackjack Bobby Crandall. His gloved hand grabbed the doorknob of the door leading to the outside hall and then stopped.

He heard footsteps rushing up the stairs.

"Which one?" Gerald Kuster whispered in the wide hall between the two apartments that filled the third floor; one to the west and the other to the east. A single light bulb shone down from the high ceiling above them casting very little illumination.

Brown looked from one door to the other realizing too late they had never considered the fact that each of these buildings always had multiple tenants on each floor. So, if Bones was actually in either apartment, they might lose their element of surprise by breaking into the wrong one. He looked to Kalita and Kuster and shrugged. He was just as much in the dark as they were.

"Aw, this is bullcrap," Kalita finally said and pointed with his Tommy gun at the door to his left. "Gerald, watch that one." Then he took two quick steps to the opposite door and kicked it with his right foot. Brown clutched his own machine gun ready for whatever happened next.

But the door didn't budge. In fact Kalita's foot had almost no affect on it whatsoever. He looked at the other two, growled and kicked it again, this time aiming for the area next to the doorknob. Supposedly that was the weakest spot. Or so he'd been told. He'd never actually kicked in a door before.

There was a cracking sound but the door remained solid and intact.

"SHIT!" He took a step back and gripping his Thompson against his side, fired a burst and blew the handle apart. The door slowly moved.

Then a woman screamed! "Aieee . . . who's there!"

"That's a woman!" Kuster stated the obvious, his shotgun still pointed at the other door.

The woman screamed a second time.

"That's the wrong door!" Brown said, now nervous. They could hear people moving around behind both doors. From the untouched one a man called out. "Whoever is out there, I'm calling the cops!"

Everything was falling apart fast. All they needed was for a bunch of folks to come storming out into the halls and see them.

"Let's get the hell out of here!" he ordered and started running down the stairs. Kalita held up his smoking machine gun and started after him cursing as he did. Finally Kuster held his shotgun against his chest and as ever, became the caboose.

"Hey, guys," he asked as they hurried down the stairwell. "What about Brother Bones?"

Brother Bones ripped open

the front door and stepped into the hallway, both .45s held in his hands and ready to unload death. Now they were pointing at a very surprised Bobby Crandall.

"AGHH!" he screamed, his hands coming up to cover his freckled face. "Sonuvabitch, Bones! You scared the shit out of me! What the hades is going on?"

Crandall dealt blackjack at the nearby Gray Owl Casino on the night shift. It being a warm night, he'd walked to and from work.

Bones kept his pistols in his gloved hands and commanded his young ally. "I'll explain later. Go back down and out the back door to get the car. Then meet me in the street."

"The street?"

"Just do what I say. There's going to be shooting."

"Alright, alright!" Used to these kind of weird demands, young Crandall started back down the stairs with the Undead Avenger on his heels. "Looks like another late night, I suppose."

He received no answer. Again, that was no surprise.

On the ground floor, Crandall headed down the corridor for the back door while Brother Bones marched quickly out the front entrance.

The three fleeing hitmen didn't see him until they were almost down the cement steps from the building's front stoop.

"Good evening, gents," his voice brought them up short and they froze on the lower steps, their weapons still clutched in their hands. And then they saw him.

He stood across the street facing them, tall in his somber overcoat with his wide brimmed hat hiding most of his white façade. Still they could all see it clearly enough as the pure white porcelain seemed to absorb the streetlamps' light and glimmer. They were looking at a skull and within its sockets there was only blackness.

"I hear you were looking for me," he held up his twin automatics. "Well, here I am."

Brown, Kalita and Kuster were transfixed, each stuck to where their feet were planted as the apparition before them was indeed a nightmare come to full blown life.

Kalita broke first and pulling up the barrel of his Thompson, he marched off the sidewalk and opened fire at the figure in black.

"YEAH!! Bring it on, Bone Man! Eat lead!"

Brother Bones merely laughed louder and started walking towards Kalita. Despite his gut wrenching fear, Kalita managed to keep his Tommy-gun steady and was gratified to see several of his shots hit the bizarre avenger. Three bullets hit Bones in the chest and staggered him, his arms flailing outward.

"Hahahaha," Kalita laughed. "How do you like them apples, Bone Man?"

Brother Bones shook himself off like a dog that had just come out of the water, his head down while he moved his big shoulders about. Then he simply raised his head and at the same time brought up his pistols and fired each. The first bullet caught Kalita in the shoulder. He began to spin around when the second projectile went through his temple.

Seeing their pal shot down, Brown and Kuster came charging

across the street, but only Michael Brown was firing. Kuster, in his rage, was holding his shotgun in front of him like some ancient battle-axe, momentarily forgetting what its real use was for.

As dozens of bullets tore up the tar in front of Brother Bones, he began laughing again, knowing full well nothing these pathetic men had could truly harm him.

Then Brown's machine-gun was empty and he stood like a fool, facing the Undead Avenger as his body started to tremble. Bones' single shot plowed through his face and he fell over to lie next to his dead compatriot, Mark Kalita.

All the while Gerald Kuster kept running forward until he was right atop the skull-faced vigilante and then his sanity returned to him. His body bumped into Brother Bones and just like that they were face to face. Sweat rolled down Kuster's brows as he now looked into those two eye-sockets. There he saw the coldest black eyes he had ever seen; at the same time he felt Bones' automatic pressing into his gut.

With tears starting to stream down his face, he made a last feeble attempt to swing his shotgun out just as both pistols barked and together blew out most of his back. Like a deck of cards, Kuster fell in on himself with a whimper and dropped to the road dead.

Brother Bones calmly put his two guns back in their shoulder rigs just as the speedy roadster came rolling around the corner. Crandall brought it to a screeching stop just in front of Brother Bones and then leaving the engine running, jumped out of the car.

"Open the trunk," Bones told him as he reached down and with one hand took hold of Gerald Kuster's jacket and lifted him off the chewed up road. He walked over to Michael Brown and picked him up with his free hand. At the back of the roadster, Crandall stood with the trunk wide open. He'd seen Bones perform such feats of strength before and none of this was new to him.

Bones tossed Kuster in the big empty trunk first and then began to drop Brown over him. As he did so something fell out of the dead man's coat and hit the ground with a clink. Crandall bent down and scooped up car keys. He looked at Bones and then over where the fancy black sedan was parked.

"You think it was theirs?" he suggested holding up the dangling keys.

"Who else in this neighborhood could afford such wheels."

"So what do we do with it?"

"Take it to a car shop and sell it for whatever you can get for it," Brother Bones said as he went to fetch Mark Kalita's corpse. "Then take the money to St. Michael's and give it to Father O'Malley. I'm sure he'll put it to good use."

"Hey, right. That's a great idea. I'll do that." Crandall stepped out of the way as his supernatural boss deposited the final body with the others. "So what are we going to do with them?"

"We are going to take them to the harbor and drop them in the bay."

After Bobby Crandall had collected the trio's weapons and dumped them in the back seat, he slid back behind the driver's wheel. Bones was already in the passenger seat and remained quiet all the way to the harbor.

At the same time Brown, Kalita and Kuster were being unceremoniously dropped into the warm waters of the Pacific, Butch Hammer was just finishing up his nightly routine in closing up the Gridiron and going home.

All the chairs had been set upside down on their tables and Old Gus was busy swiping a wet mop around the wooden floor pulling the bucket-on-wheels as he went. His peg leg made a tapping sound whenever he took a step.

"Well, I'm out of here," Hammer declared as he threw on his short-waist jacket and newsboy cap by the front door. "We'll see you tomorrow morning, Gus. Don't forget to lock up."

"Ain't done it yet," the cantankerous old sailor fired back. "Don't plan on starting now."

The old fellow stopped moving the mop for a minute and scratched his chin as if perplexed by something. "Butch, I been thinking about what I told them three fellahs earlier tonight."

"What, about where to find Brother Bones?"

"Uh-huh. It got me to thinking just now . . . you know, how they got house numbers done up a certain fixed way."

"What do you mean? Like all the even numbers are on one side of the street and the odds are on the other?"

"Right." Old Gus looked at his boss and said. "Been thinking I might have given them guys the wrong number, Butch. I told 'em it was twenty-six. But the more I think about it, I think it was really twenty-seven."

"Oh, well, I don't think it's any big deal. You can tell them the right one next time they come in."

"Yeah, I suppose. Okay, boss. Have a good night."

"You too, Gus. Bye."

Old Gus watched his employer close the door behind him and through the plate glass window go walking off into the night. He shook his head for a second at how fuzzy his old brain got sometimes.

Then he began whistling a rowdy tune he'd learned when he was a young man in Calcutta. He danced with his swaying mop across the wet floor.

↙ ↘

A professional writer for over thirty-five years, **Ron Fortier** has worked on comic book projects such as The Hulk, Popeye, Rambo and Peter Pan; with The Green Hornet and The Terminator (with Alex Ross) being his two most popular series. He penned two TSR fantasy novels with Ardath Mayhar, and in 2001 had his first play, a World War II romantic comedy, produced.

Ron currently writes and produces pulp novels and short stories for a wide range of publishers; and has several movie scripts floating around Hollywood looking for a home. If that isn't enough, he also writes Pulp Fiction Reviews, online at: pulpfictionreviews.blogspot.com

A devoted grandfather of six, at 68, Ron is thrilled to be part of the new web-comic evolution. Part of this joy is in the realization of a life long dream, that of becoming a pulp writer. For news about Ron's many projects visit airship27.com

---

Like The Digest Enthusiast page on Facebook to add updates on the world of digest magazines to your FB feed.
facebook.com/thedigestenthusiast/

SINISTER BARRIER
By ERIC FRANK RUSSELL

Galaxy
SCIENCE FICTION
NOVEL NO. I.
25¢

Galaxy Novel #1 1950 cover by David Stone

The Galaxy Science Fiction Novels
Article by Steve Carper

"For five miles straight as an arrow, the gleaming metal track lay along the face of the desert. It pointed to the northwest across the dead heart of the continent and to the ocean beyond. Over this land, once the home of the aborigines, many strange shapes had risen, roaring, in the last generation. The greatest and strangest of them all lay at the head of the launching track along which it was to hurtle into the sky."
Prelude to Space by Arthur C. Clarke

World War II threw onto front pages a number of marvels that once were the province of science fiction, conferring on the scorned and infantilized field an instant dollop of respectability. After almost universally ignoring the genre, mainstream publishers were quick to throw a handful of relevant titles into print, though none deigned to plaster the suspect words "science fiction" on covers or flaps, no matter how apt the description might be. Paperback publishers, slavishly following every sellable trend, followed. That included digest publishers. Bonded, Leslie Charteris' California press meant to reprint Saint stories, republished Malcolm Jameson's 1943 *Startling Stories* novel "The Giant

Atom" under the title *Atomic Bomb* (#10-A) in 1945. Handi-Books reprinted the atomic war novel *The Murder of the U.S.A.* (#62) by Will F. Jenkins (who wrote f&sf as Murray Leinster) in 1947. Century Adventures tried Harold Sherman's more forthrightly genre original novel *The Green Man: A Visitor from Outer Space* (#104) in 1946.

By 1950 fans tried to rectify the situation by launching more than a dozen small presses to print nothing but f&sf and trumpet the fact loudly. Their books appeared in hardcovers, so that for the first time f&sf titles could be found in bookstores and be purchased by libraries, on an equal basis with any mainstream book. Economic necessity meant they were also the price of mainstream hardcovers, a steep for the day $2.50 or $3.00. A small but intensely loyal audience bought them. Small presses could issue runs in small numbers; paperback publishers couldn't. Not a single paperback line devoted to original or reprint f&sf novels existed.

When the Italian company Edizioni Mondiale (World Editions in the U.S.) offered Horace L. Gold a chance to address the exploitable niche, he jumped in with both feet: a high-paying f&sf magazine to lure the best writers simultaneous with a line of reprint science fiction novels in digest form to cater to that desperate but price-sensitive audience. It's obvious which one should have become successful. The number of f&sf magazines had zoomed to match the boom. Michael Ashley pegs it going from 8 in 1946 to 20 in 1950. Lester del Rey, with different definitions, claims 25 different titles put out a total of 110 issues that year. Yet *Galaxy Science Fiction* magazine (*Galaxy*) was an instant success that was to define high-end science fiction for the 1950s while the Galaxy Science Fiction Novels line (Novels) was a depressing failure that is almost lost to memory. David L. Rosheim's obsessive 300+ page story-by-story history, *Galaxy Magazine: The Dark and the Light Years*, devotes all of three paragraphs to the Novels. What went wrong? Everything.

Despite the cold logic of economics textbooks, advantages can accrue to one more of the same. *Galaxy* was immediately findable and understandable. Newsstands tended to group magazines by subject, so that a reader glancing at the racks would see a multitude of science fiction, probably in a familiar and easily remembered corner of the stand. A new title announced what it was to the most casual customer. Presentation and contents and price determined whether a reader picked it up and took it home. *Galaxy* had the best package in f&sf. That first, October 1950, issue had a stunning astronomical cover by David Stone, enabled by Gold's shrewd use of Champion Kromekote, bright white, slick, calendared stock that made the colors appear to rise above the page three-dimensionally. Through sheer luck the October issues of competing digests *Astounding*, *F&SF*, and *Imagination* had fantasy themes, subtly less appealing in a technological age. A peek inside revealed an all-star contents page: Clifford D. Simak, Theodore Sturgeon, Katherine MacLean, Richard Matheson, Fritz Leiber, Fredric Brown, Isaac Asimov, and Willy Ley, all available for the standard magazine price of 25¢.

In stark contrast, a science fiction digest novel line had no obvious place at a newsstand. It probably would sit with all the other digests in a stack or rack. Readers who took the time to go through a stack might notice that the spine of #1 was printed upside down, hardly an inducement. Neither was the cover. Although text stated "Galaxy Science Fiction Novel No. 1," the cover art did not grab attention or indicate genre. Gold instituted a firm cover policy banning aliens, monsters, imperiled near-naked damsels, or other clichéd f&sf tropes. He wanted to lift the softcovers into par with the new found respectability of their contents. That meant covers that didn't scream science fiction. A portrait of Depression-era oppressed-working-man slice of life, unrecognizably drawn by the same David Stone who so beautified *Galaxy* #1, whispered untruthfully that the bleakest of contemporary tales lay inside Novel #1, *Sinister Barrier*, by Eric Frank Russell. A reprint of a reprint, the tale first appeared as a "complete novel" in the very first issue of *Unknown*, March 1939, John W. Campbell's fantasy companion magazine to *Astounding*. Fantasy Press, one of those small, specialized post-war f&sf publishers, offered it in a revised and greatly expanded hardcover edition in 1948. Gold printed "The Complete Book Version, Unabridged" on the title page: the Wikipedia entry for *Sinister Barrier* reports it as abridged as of this writing, but I can't find any confirmation of that. (Similarly, the Internet Speculative Fiction Database [ISFDB] says of the 1943 British hardback "Text differs substantially from the original magazine version published in *Unknown* in March 1939. [Currey]" which is the exact opposite of what L. W. Currey actually says in his *Science Fiction and Fantasy Authors*.)

Campbell started *Unknown* ostensibly to print modern fantasy, but mostly because too many writers submitted stories to *Astounding* that didn't fit his strict interpretation of science fiction. *Sinister Barrier* is set in the far future (i.e. the year 2015) for no reason other than that the future is where science fiction is set. The concept reveals the thinness of the line between fantasy and science fiction: humans are and have always been the property of a race of normally invisible aliens, the Vitons, who feed on our emotions just as we milk cows. This ultimate conspiracy theory conveniently addresses every oddity in the history of mankind, from saints' visions to world wars. Contemporary readers were prodded to remember the late Charles Fort, the first omniconspiracy theorist, whose four books collected thousands of weird happenings and, in just asking questions style, wondered whether aliens might be responsible. Russell continued collecting after Fort's death: amusingly almost all his newspaper clippings from "one hundred and fifty years" happen to be dated 1938. Although Fort was hugely popular in the f&sf community, his books had been out of print for a decade and his rejection of mainstream science was at odds with the near-worship of scientific achievements prevalent in 1950. Perhaps Gold was attracted by the intense tone of very contemporary paranoia Russell dragged onto every page.

"*When you see this world riddled with suspicion, rotten with*

Galaxy Novel #2 1951 cover by Paul Callé

conflicting ideas, staggering beneath the burden of preparation for war, you can be certain that the harvest time is drawing near—a harvest for others. Not for you, not for you—you are only the poor, bleeding suckers whose lot it is to be pushed around. **The harvest is for others!**" [p70. emphasis in original]

Well written and compelling—until it descends into the standard plucky-humans-fight-back with science-y word-driven fol-de-rol (if you didn't guess that the humans win with hyperbolic polarization, shame on you)—to modern eyes it's an extremely odd choice of an inaugural book for the Novels. Not least because nothing inside the covers indicates what the Novels were intended to be. The front and end pages are blank, as are the inside covers, normally the spaces in which publishers extolled their coming wares. The back cover is an ad for *Galaxy*, reprinted from the back cover of *Galaxy*'s first issue. Out of that context, it lacks a certain something. To be exact, it lacks the information that *Galaxy* was a magazine. Or an address for subscribing to it. Or any possible way to get more from those unknown and unnamed Galaxy people except to wait and hope to stumble upon a Galaxy-named object on a newsstand.

People reading *Galaxy* received much more information. An ad for *Sinister Barrier* on the inside back cover of the first issue called it "a complete, unexpurgated novel, exactly as it appeared in book version, in GALAXY Science Fiction's bimonthly companion reprint magazine." [italics in original] Those interested could send in $1.50 for "six future novels in *Galaxy's* exciting series." Amazingly, the ad gave no way to order *Sinister Barrier* itself. Neither did a separate ad on p. 158, which told potential buyers to get it "At Any Newsstand." If you liked *Galaxy*, the ad read, "You'll want GALAXY *Science Fiction Novels*! Published bimonthly in Similar Format, GALAXY *Science Fiction Novels* present the finest, most popular book-length stories. . ." Apparently "popular" was a code word for "previously published." Gold waited until the third issue of *Galaxy* before mentioning the Novels in his editorials. He asked readers to write in and answer the question "What books would you like to see reprinted?" In the only hint as to selection criteria we ever get, Gold continued, "None, by the way, will be reprints of books already published at 25¢." Not much of a limiting factor, given how few had. That avalanche of reprint titles would be seen later in the 1950s, so Gold had a lead, although others technically had the same idea even earlier. Mary Gnaedinger was currently editing three separate magazines—*A. Merritt's Fantasy Magazine, Famous Fantastic Mysteries,* and *Fantastic Novels Magazine*—with a classic novel as a lead entry. All three were pulp-sized magazines. So was *Two Complete Science Fiction Adventures*, whose first issue, dated Winter 1950, reprinted Isaac Asimov's *Pebble in the Sky* and L. Ron Hubbard's "The Kingslayer." The Novels were alone in limiting the contents to a single work in digest format, yet that made them less like a magazine and more like digest-sized novels, a different beast, one almost designed to confuse both vendors and potential customers.

If the beginning had been inauspicious and fumbled, at least *Sinister Barrier* had contemporary pizazz. The next book was a saga of super-science, of brave Earthmen fighting hideous aliens with a weapon that can (and does) destroy the moon, a nostalgic exercise in Gosh-wow science fiction of the sort that *Galaxy* had pledged to obliterate from the field. Jack Williamson's *The Legion of Space* first saw print as a six-part serial in *Astounding* in 1934. It too had seen hardcover publication by Fantasy Press, in 1947, without updating. Williamson held legendary status, true, and must have sold well; Fantasy Press had published the Legion's sequel stories as *The Cometeers* earlier in 1950. Whatever potential the Novels reprint had as a sure-fire hit was mitigated by Paul Callé's cover art, which strips out the space adventure for a seeming jungle yarn. Gold wanted adults to buy *Galaxy*; tricking adults into buying *The Legion of Space* took effort. That *Galaxy* and the Novels were intended to be complementary

Galaxy Novel #3 1951 cover by Bunch

approaches became explicit as each inside cover had ads, one of which shouted that the Novels could be delivered to you at a Christmas bargain of a mere $1.25 for six releases.

The inside front cover of *Legion of Space* promised Hal Clement's *Needle*, a 1949 *Astounding* serial, for the next selection. It went to mainstream giant Doubleday instead. Worse, in Gold's eyes, was that Street & Smith, *Astounding*'s publisher, had a new policy of purchasing the reprint (second serial) rights for novels they serialized and was reluctant to let them go for the flat $500 fee Gold offered. That added to a series of grievances Gold had against *Astounding*'s editor John W. Campbell and led to a bitter feud lasting as long as Gold remained *Galaxy*'s editor.

Gold hurriedly filled the slot with the existential opposite of super-science, an original novel set in a recognizable future. It had everything—a rising young star as its author, cutting-edge contemporary subject matter, a realistic style that eschewed Gosh-wow, an astronomical cover that for once indicated the lure of the contents, the true first edition of the first novel ever published by a name destined to achieve world renown. Arthur C. Clarke's *Prelude to Space* (#3) fell into Gold's lap for the least likely possible reason: everybody else in the field had rejected it.

We have a nearly perfect source for Clarke's side of it, the diaries of British writer Bill Temple, a fellow member of the British Interplanetary Society who was once Clarke's flatmate in London. The relevant entry, as transcribed in the fanzine *Relapse* #17, Spring 2010:

16 November 1950; "This morning Ego rang to tell me of another sale by Meredith for him—his novel PRELUDE TO SPACE, a pocket edition of 150,000 copies, he getting a cent a copy and 750 dollars (over £250) advance. Only fair to add it was after 3 years' hawking & over 30 rejections. But Ego always gets there in the end if he doesn't, as is more frequent, do it right away."

Yes, Clarke's nickname in the f&sf/rocketry community was Ego. Considering the competition, this may be the most impressive feat of his fabled career.

Temple's diary is the only evidence for the Novels print run and that Gold paid more money for original novels than reprints, as well he should. Unfortunately, there is a piece of counter-evidence that normally would be equally convincing. It comes from Gold himself, taken from an essay written for the anthology *Galaxy: Thirty Years of Innovative Science Fiction*:

One manuscript that came my way was Prelude to Space, by Arthur C. Clarke. I read it and wanted to use it, but I could see that it wouldn't break up into a serial. So I asked Clarke's agent, Scott Meredith, if we could run it as a Galaxy Novel, warning that all we could pay was five hundred bucks. He said sure. I said, "Why do you say sure so quickly? It's a good story and you should think it over." He said, "It's been kicking around for three years. A publisher's a publisher." So I got it for five hundred, and as soon as it came out everybody realized they'd passed up a hell of a bet.

For our purposes, the telling phrase is "a publisher's a publisher." How low in the pecking order must the Novels have been in Meredith's eyes? Merely finding 30 possible publishers for rejections was a superhuman feat in the late 1940s, and he must have sent off the manuscript to every start-up the moment he heard of it through the grapevine. For Clarke, the fortuitous timing was perfection, the boost a man with only a dozen or so American story sales needed. *Prelude to Space* would be the only Novel to be reviewed in *Galaxy*, the first paperback original to achieve that status. "Recommended for readers whose taste goes beyond Perry Mason," wrote Groff Conklin, very drily. Even f&sf magazines discriminated against paperback originals then. Clarke's debut had to be exceptionally strong to overcome that prejudice. The book also attracted mainstream attention, as in a newspaper review whose writer spent more than half the article saying what the book was not, i.e. not a collection of Gosh-wow clichés for semi-illiterates.

Gold felt the same way, if we go by the inside front cover blurb:

> You'll find here no wicked wenches seducing secrets from innocent engineers . . . no enemy sabotage attempts . . . no gadgeteers putting together items from the corner hardware store to be the first to conquer space . . . or any of the other machine-made devices of juvenile science fiction. [ellipses in original]

He might as well have been summarizing *Legion of Space*.

Prelude to Space was labeled "A Compellingly Realistic Novel of Interplanetary Flight," an achievement no more than a handful of humans were capable of in 1951. No novel of the period comes closer to fulfilling Campbell's dream submission: "I want the kind of story that could be printed in a magazine of the year two thousand A.D. as a contemporary adventure story. No gee-whiz, just take the technology for granted." Clarke's reportorial account of the first moon launch is uncanny in the hindsight of the Mercury and Apollo programs. Although every minor detail is wrong, the overall thrust of the technology, the selection of the astronauts, the frenzied and often irrational reactions of the public, and the visionary combination of art and science in the participants are instantly familiar.

How could so perspicacious a view of the future be rejected by every editor in the field, presumably including Campbell? The only conceivable answer is that Clarke deliberately redacted adventure from the story. A few technical glitches, a modicum of tension among contrasting personalities, are all that stand in the way of an inevitable ending. Nothing read less like science fiction in 1951 than a compellingly realistic portrayal of building a moon rocket in 1978. Despite an epilog set twenty years later, the book properly ends with the launch of *Prometheus*; interplanetary flight is told but not shown. Nothing read more like science fiction in 1951, though, if we move the focus to its almost completely white, male, Anglo-Saxon cast. Despite the global collaboration the technical crew and the astronauts are American or British, with the flavoring of one Frenchman. He is limited to a single line of dialog, less than the one female, a nitwit reporter. The German scientists who did so much for the real space effort are a shadow in passing. At the end a minor walk-on named Achmet Singh has a role, keeping the exoticism within the British Empire. It has to be said that Clarke got this prediction correct: You can search images of Apollo mission control and count on the fingers of one hand those who are not white, male, or wearing a tie.

Prelude to Space and another 1951 original novel, *Sands of Mars*, gave Clarke status in the field and allowable exoticism to the mainstream audience when the nonfiction blockbuster *The Exploration of Space* followed, the perfect book for the mass audience in the budding age of rocketry and a lead selection of the Book-of-the-Month Club for July 1952. "Clarke . . . is not a science-fictioneer," Ellis D. Roberts reassured his audience in the Carbondale *Southern Illinoisan* for June 30, 1952. No, he was a sensation. In 1953 *Prelude to Space* went from obscure digest paperback to hardcover publication in Britain and in 1954 Gnome Press, another

Galaxy Novel #6 1951

of the specialty publishers, made it its third Clarke title in four years. Mass-market paperbacks hit newsstands in both countries later that year, some of the eight books in print for Ego, getting there not in the end but impossibly quickly. The Novels edition had little to do with that fame. For collectors it remains undoubtedly the cheapest true first printing of a first novel by a world-class writer in or out of the genre.

After the coup with an original novel, Gold marked time, deep time, going back to 1925 and 1929 for S. Fowler Wright's *The Amphibians* (#4) and its sequel *The World Below* (#5), neatly addressing several of his problems at once. The books themselves were classics, called by Everett F. Bleiler "undoubtedly the major work of genre science-fiction between early Wells and the moderns." The two had in 1949 been published in a single volume by Shasta: Publishers, one more 1940s small press, at a hefty price of $3.50, creating a demand for a cheaper paperback edition. Both volumes were short, allowing him to cut the number of pages from 160 (ten 16-page signatures) to 128 (eight 16-page signatures), saving money at a time when the Korean War had suddenly sent paper costs soaring. As a philosophical allegory set in the very far future based on the first two books of Dante's Divine Comedy (nobody knows why Wright didn't finish the trilogy although it's telling that he had translated *Inferno* and *Purgatorio* but never got to *Paradiso*), they raised the tone of the Novels from Williamson and justified the use of the studiously non-genre covers by Paul Callé.

Then came two original novels in a row, *The Alien* by Raymond F. Jones (#6) and *Empire* by Clifford D. Simak (#7). Both had 160 pages but a higher price of 35¢, a concession to reality that Gold could never let drop. The alien of the title of Jones' book is found buried deep in an asteroid, the remains of a planet that exploded 500,000 years ago, creating the asteroid belt. That impossible cosmology is par for the book, which has its archaeologist heroes battle the weaponized brain of the alien by hopping into a convenient-but-never-before-mentioned faster-than-light starship and zooming to another planet to bring back the only weapon in the universe that can defeat him. That weapon is also mental, provided by the hero's girlfriend, a surgeon so incredibly talented that she figures out how to transplant an alien organ into his brain just by looking at it. Fittingly, the only science that Jones cares about is Alfred Korzybski's General Semantics, which posited that humans can only perceive the world through verbal abstractions created in the brain.

With its non-existent characterization, thin yet melodramatic plot, and ludicrous science, *The Alien* is a perfect example of what contemporaries pointed to when they called f&sf a sub-literary genre. Its concern, however superficial, for social problems makes the novel a smidge better than *Empire*, which has less characterization, a thinner plot, and even more ludicrous science. The villain is the Interplanetary Power corporation, whose monopoly of a power supply makes them the de facto dictators of the solar system. Two brilliant scientists find an alternate power source that can do literally anything: two-way transmissions of light and sound, manipulation of objects anywhere in the universe, teleportation, faster-than-light travel, and much more critical to the plot. The bad guy's scientist manages to duplicate this effect all by himself. (The three also personally build all their inventions from scratch, while spying on each other constantly. Nobody in any novel has ever needed less sleep.) A series of awesome battles stretch from Earth into deepest space, with the good guys winning, a revolution tearing down the dictatorship, and an all-powerful superweapon left dangling over everyone's heads. Like *The Alien*, *Empire* would make a terrific modern superhero comic book, precisely why it makes for an execrable serious novel.

Such a plot sounds bizarre coming from the pen of Simak, one of the most humanistic writers in the genre. Fortunately, it wasn't his. A teenaged Campbell wrote it as super-science back in the 1920s. It

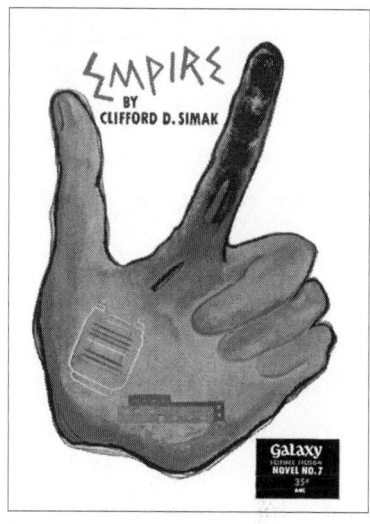

Galaxy Novel #7 1951

would have been his first sale, but didn't live up even to Gernsbackian standards. He gave the manuscript to Simak, just getting started on writing full-length novels, to rewrite and update with the intention of publishing it in *Astounding*. At the age of 40, with thirteen years of editing under his belt, Campbell knew twaddle when he saw it. He rejected his own still-unpublishable book. Simak wrote, "*Empire* was essentially a rewrite of John's plot. I may have taken a few of the ideas and action, but I didn't use any of his words. And I certainly tried to humanize his characters." What could they have been like before? (There's also not a single female character with a line of dialog.) Gold probably ran it mostly as part of his feud with Campbell, although it surely was a sop to Simak to stay on as a *Galaxy* author.

Other than as a resume credit, neither book redounded to fame and glory for anyone involved. Nobody took note. Neither *The Alien* nor

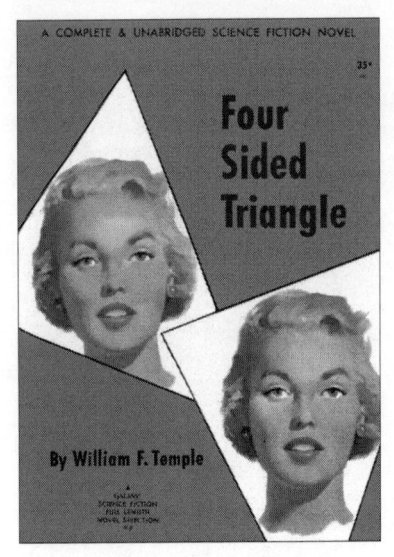

Galaxy Novel #9 1952 cover by Richard Powers

Empire has a single review recorded in the ISFDB. *Empire*, despite Simak's Hall of Fame status, went more than 50 years before any English-language reprinting; *The Alien* had two low-level mass-market editions in that span. Worse, both Novels had pages in which paragraphs were printed out of order, a fatal lack of proofreading making poor reads entirely incomprehensible in spots.

Gold gave up experimenting and went back to reprints of proven quality, mixing newer works with old. Although the Novels couldn't have made much money they probably didn't lose any either. Gold might have used them merely as a platform from which to advertise *Galaxy*. Or maybe his new publisher, Robert Guinn, who was also his printer and source of paper stock, felt that keeping his presses busy while moving paper out the door was sufficient rationale.

Odd John (#8), Olaf Stapledon's 1935 classic about a mutant supergenius, finished out 1951. William F. Temple's *Four-Sided Triangle* (#9) lost its hyphen on the cover and spine while Jay Franklin's *The Rat Race* (#10) saw the "The" go missing likewise and his name change to J. Franklin on the spine. It's hard not to think that nobody paid close attention to any fine details of the Novels, new or old. The three books, wildly different in tone and style, nevertheless belong to the same subgenre that today is called slipstream: each lives in their current mainstream world with an impossibility added. That separates them from Russell and Clarke, whose works are genre because they write of an impossibility to which a world is appended to enable a story.

Temple is the same Bill Temple of the Clarke quote and he's connected to Stapledon in two ways. Not only were both British, giving British writers six of the first nine slots in the Novels, an oddity in the intensely chauvinistic world of American f&sf, but his 1949 book from mainstream publisher John Long also starts with a supergenius prodigy. One that invents a matter duplicator that works quite well on humans, so that two men in love with the same woman have an instant solution to their dilemma. Franklin, a pseudonym for the newspaperman John Franklin Carter, who had earlier written a string of mysteries under the name Diplomat, also deals in problems of identity in *The Rat Race*. The protagonist's problem is that his consciousness is placed into another man's body when a thorium bomb goes off under his feet. His antagonist lands in that man's dog's brain. Neither stays in place. Although it had been serialized in the mainstream and high-paying magazine *Collier's* in 1947, no mainstream publisher ever touched it and the hardcover appeared from small press Fantasy Publishing Company, Inc. (entirely unconnected to the Fantasy Press). Contrarily, Wilson "Bob" Tucker's first sf novel, *The City in the Sea* (#11) had been published in 1951 by the mainstream house Rinehart, his mystery publisher, although the far future post-apocalyptic setting was overtly science fiction. For their original publications, Groff Conklin in *Galaxy* heaped superlatives on Temple, imprecations on Franklin, and faint praise on Tucker. No matter. All vanished from American publishing with the exception of a 2001 reprint of *Triangle*.

After reading *The Alien* and *Empire*, *The City in the Sea* hit me like a sorbet-like mid-meal palate cleanser. Although not well thought of, as is normal for first novels, *The City in the Sea*—a title taken from a poem by Poe—should be far more famous than it is. Thousands of years after an atomic war, Britain has a small civilization at the spear-throwing level. They've re-colonized America but are content to hug the Atlantic until a native appears to lead them past the Appalachians. What appears to be a standard set-up isn't. All the leaders and soldiers are women in this matriarchy. For perhaps the first time in the field of f&sf, an entire story, an entire civilization, is told through the eyes of women, non-stereotyped, competent, individualized women. Tucker's characters are adults with the concomitant complicated adult feelings and relationships, a portent of the fine writer he would become. His flaw in this novel is that of Clarke's; the reportorial tone dumps adventure for minute descriptions. In place of frantic plot twists and space battles that grow huger by the page in defiance of physics, Tucker presents the consequences of the ice caps melting and rearranging the coastline of America and a discussion of biology that hangs together 65 years later.

The last of only four releases in 1952 had a slightly brighter future. Sam Merwin, Jr. was a well-known editor in the field who decided to return to full-time writing. *The House of Many Worlds* (#12) was also his first sf novel after, yes, several mysteries. Mysteries were the only legitimized genre in the 1940s; they appeared from mainstream publishers, received decent advances, and had high probabilities of being published in cheap hardcover or paperback reprints, giving authors a continuing stream of money. F&sf had the barest shadow of that life cycle, and wouldn't match it for aftersales for another decade. Mainstream giant Doubleday published the novel in 1951 (almost simultaneously with its appearance in the September *Startling Stories*) and made it a selection of its Science Fiction Book Club in 1953, giving it visibility that the Novels clearly lacked, probably the reason it went on to accrue a couple of mass-market reprints. Watchers watch alternate worlds through a portal but, unlike Marvel's The Watcher, they interfere for the greater good. The hero team is a partnership between a man and a woman, continuing the short streak started with Tucker. (The woman duplicated by Temple is quite a woman, but she does nothing but stand around and have

Galaxy Novel #14 1953 cover by Richard Powers

men fall insanely in love with her.)

The first Novel of 1953, *Seeds of Life* (#13), came to Gold by way of the Fall 1931 *Amazing Stories Quarterly* and Fantasy Press. John Taine hid the identity of Eric Temple Bell, one of the most prominent scientists ever to work in the field. His villain gets superpowers from an exploding X-ray tube, a plot that must be firmly implanted in Stan Lee's subconscious. Scottish author J. Leslie's Mitchell's *Three Go Back* (#15) was just a year younger, and had been reprinted by Mary Gnaedinger in *Famous Fantastic Mysteries*, December 1943. Back to first novels with *Pebble in the Sky* (#14) from the ever-clicking typewriter of Isaac Asimov, even though, as mentioned above, it had already seen a 25¢ reprint. (Campbell had rejected it before Doubleday picked it up. Gold must have enjoyed this third finger thrust at his judgement.) Two more books from *Two Complete Science-Adventure Books*

would rapidly appear: James Blish's first novel ran as *Sword of Xota* in the Summer 1951 issue and was reprinted in the Novels as *Warriors of Day* (#16) and Jack Williamson's *The Humanoids* (#21), originally a 1948 *Astounding* serial, had also seen a reprint there in the Spring 1952 issue. Apparently pulp magazines didn't count as paperbacks for reprint purposes. I don't know if this confluence of first novels was a deliberate contrivance of Gold's or forced upon him by his tiny budget and the ever-increasing number of competitors for name authors. Both Merwin and Blish saw their second books picked up as well, in 1953 and 1954. *Jack of Eagles* (#19) was Blish's first hardcover, published by the mainstream Greenberg Publishers in 1952. Merwin's *Killer to Come* (#22) had a hardcover edition from the mainstream Abelard Press in 1953.

The City in the Sea is the last book to proclaim "Complete and Unabridged" on the cover. Despite an increase to 176 pages (11 signatures) for *Seeds of Life*, Algis Budrys, the newly hired editorial assistant at *Galaxy*, needed to cut *Pebble in the Sky* to get it into 10 signatures. From *Three Go Back* onward, all of the Novels were limited to 128 pages (8 signatures). A thicker and presumably cheaper grade of paper also kicks in, with these books bulking larger than the early books with 25% more pages. That didn't last. Nothing lasted. From the evidence Guinn then on used whatever inexpensive grade of paper he had lying around and printed the Novels using whatever idle press could be pressed into service. The releases varied by millimeters in height, width, and depth from one book

Galaxy Novel #15 1953 cover by Richard Powers

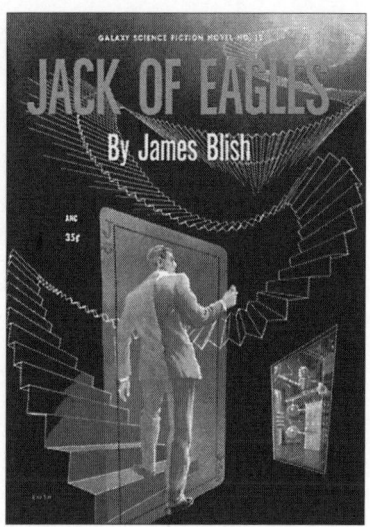

Galaxy Novel #19 1953 cover by Ed Emshwiller

to the next. Looking at the collection from the reverse resembles a topographic map. The pure whiteness of the much-touted Kromekote cover stock also vanished, replaced with a variety of papers that turned almost as brown as the text pages. Inside cover ads mostly disappeared after #13, though #23, 24, 30, and 31 had them. Books that ended on page 128 had no inside sales pitches at all and some of those had a *Galaxy* ad on the back, so no subscription information for the Novels appeared anywhere in the book.

The Novels suffered because *Galaxy* did. The overwhelming success of the magazine gave Gold visions of empire. Not only did he manage to squeeze seven Novels into 1953, he started a UK edition of *Galaxy* and founded *Beyond Fantasy Fiction*, the fantasy magazine he had wanted from the beginning, with a UK edition of that appearing late in the year with a January 1954 cover date. His timing was bad, but he wasn't alone. More f&sf magazine titles, 36 of them, were released in 1953 than any other year. An oversaturated market began to crumble. Small presses like FPCI and Shasta stopped publishing in 1953; although each would try to come back they had essentially died. Mainstream publishers, both hardcover and mass-market paperback, moved to take over a field floundering under the weight of amateurs and opportunists. Publishers began to abandon the very notion of digest-sized novels. Writers of f&sf were caught in a squeeze of their own. With fewer short fiction slots available, fewer good new authors had a place to break into the field. They had to learn how to write coherent novels that weren't designed as serials or successions of novelettes in magazines, but the mainstream opened only so far and was dominated by older authors who already had names that sold. The quality of *Galaxy* fell sharply as the decade

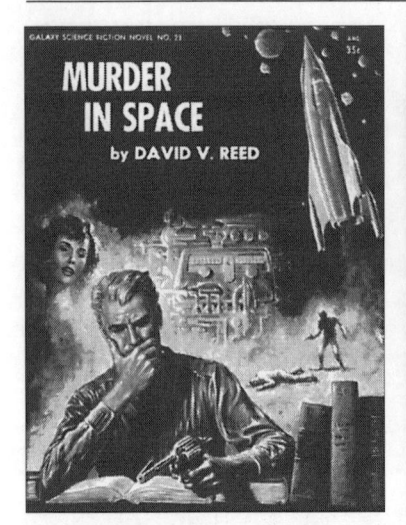

Galaxy Novel #23 1954 cover by Ed Emshwiller

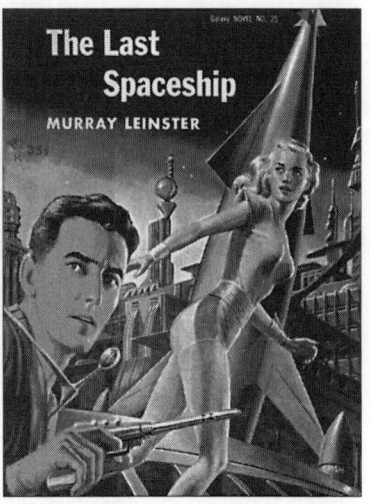

Galaxy Novel #25 1955 cover by Ed Emshwiller

progressed. Publishing, like virtually every field, wobbles between boom and bust. The Novels staggered on through the bust, increasingly irrelevant and invisible. Only four appeared in 1954, two in 1955, two in 1956, three in 1957, and one in 1958.

Gold mined Merwin's run as editor of *Startling* for three books by old pros, *Well of the Worlds* (#17) by Lewis Padgett (March 1952), *City at World's End* (#18) by Edmond Hamilton (July 1950), and *The Black Galaxy* (#20) by Murray Leinster (March 1949). The first two appeared in 1953, the third in 1954. That year also saw Jack Williamson's *The Humanoids* (#21), a 1948 serial from *Astounding* that saw hardcovers from mainstream publisher Simon & Schuster, and David V. Reed's *Murder in Space* (#23), which first appeared in the May 1944 *Amazing Stories* and like so many other of the Novels never saw another English-language printing for 50 years. L. Sprague de Camp's *Lest Darkness Falls* (#24), an oft-reprinted classic first published in the December 1939 *Unknown*, and Leinster's *The Last Spaceship* (#25), an original 1949 novel from mainstream publisher Frederick Fell, were the only two that appeared in 1955. Two more familiar names were the sole books in 1956, Padgett's *Chessboard Planet* (#26), a 1946 serial in *Astounding* under the name "The Fairy Chessmen," and *Tarnished Utopia* (#27) by Malcolm Jameson, from the March 1942 *Startling*, ending a run of ten straight covers by Ed Emshwiller.

Of similar age were the 1957 offerings. Leo and Diane Dillon provided distinctive covers for Fritz Leiber's *Destiny Times Three* (#28), a 1945 *Astounding* serial, and for L. Ron Hubbard's *Fear* (#29), yet another from *Unknown*, dating to July 1940. Like *Four-Sided Triangle*, Fletcher Pratt's *Double Jeopardy* (#30) has a cover with twin blondes and a matter duplicator is again the reason. Despite also calling the machine a Reproducer,

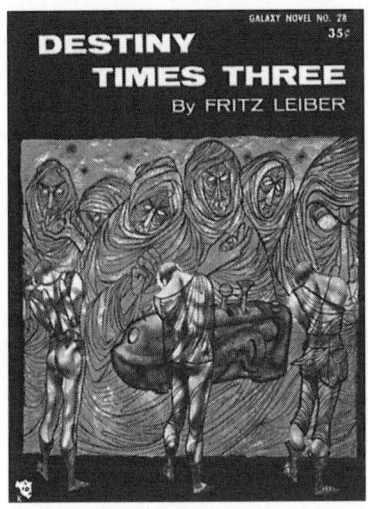

Galaxy Novel #28 1957

it's impossible to accuse Pratt's book, based on two connected tales from *Thrilling Wonder Stories* in 1952, and put into hardcovers by Doubleday, of plagiarism so different is every other detail.

The very last book in the Novels, the only digest from 1958, draws together a number of threads that

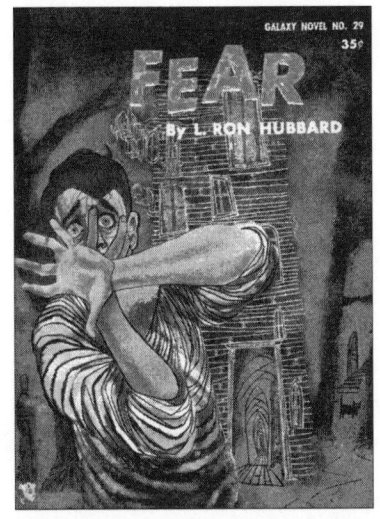

Galaxy Novel #29 1954 cover by Leo and Diane Dillon

Galaxy Novel #31 1958

run through the later years of the series. "The publication of **Shambleau** is an event that readers have been demanding for years," read the back cover blurb [bold in original], not exactly truthfully. The story made C. L. Moore an instant star when it appeared in the November 1933 *Weird Tales*. Donald Wollheim reprinted it in a cheap digest form, *Avon Fantasy Reader* 7, 1948, and Kendell Foster Crossen included it in his 1951 hardback anthology *Adventures in Tomorrow*. The small press also had its crack at it in 1953 when Gnome published it as one of seven Moore stories in *Shambleau and Others*. "Shambleau" is obviously not a novel. It's not even a long novelette. What is revealed nowhere unless you actually read through the Novel is that the volume is bulked out by mining two of the other three unrelated novelettes also starring Northwest Smith from the Gnome collection. Both "Black Thirst" and "The Tree of Life" are longer than "Shambleau," but lacked its brand name. Martin Greenberg's

Gnome, the last survivor of the 1940s boom and unrelated to Greenberg Publishers, was the supplier of choice in the Novels' sunset years. *Destiny Times Three* had appeared as one of its *Five Science Fiction Novels* omnibus; *Fear* was included in *Typewriter in the Sky / Fear*; and *Chessboard Planet* had been half of *Tomorrow and Tomorrow and the Fairy Chessmen*. Moore was also the first and only woman to be published in the Novels though this wasn't her first appearance. As was an open secret in the field by then, "Lewis Padgett" was a joint pseudonym for Catherine Moore and her husband Henry Kuttner. Readers who were not insiders may not have known this, especially because the Padgett books had a distressing habit of being reprinted credited only to Kuttner. Nor did the laudatory blurb give any indication that C. L. Moore was a woman. One other oddity: the copyright date was given as 1953, from the Gnome edition, hiding the fact that all three stories were a quarter-century old. Only one of the last dozen Novels truly dated from the 1950s.

All the major digest-novel lines died in 1958, and the Novels were no exception. Gold continued the series with four mass-market-sized paperbacks in 1958, three of whom were reprints of fairly recent full-length books. They simply disappeared and are almost forgotten except by a few collectors. Gold then turned the distribution over to Beacon Books for 11 more titles, but Beacon had been exclusively a publisher of soft-core "sleaze" books and neither audience wanted or expected f&sf from it. Those are equally invisible except to the most dedicated completists.

In an article almost two decades later, "Looking Aft," Gold would write, "As for the Galaxy SF Novel reprints—they weren't handled right as packages, being more like numbered magazines than paperbacks. I got that go-ahead just as the paperback market broke, but it was too late." We'll never know if anybody else could have done them better: nobody else tried. An all f&sf paperback line in 1950 was at least twenty years ahead of possible profitability. The Novels were a footnote to *Galaxy*'s half-decade of success, just as they were to the careers of any of the individual authors. F&SF began to grow up in the 1950s. The Novels exemplify those growing pains.

The ISFDB has full bibliographical information on its Galaxy Novels page: http://www.isfdb.org/cgi-bin/pubseries.cgi?176

The past is **Steve Carper's** future. He created the Flying Cars and Food Pill website: flyingcarsandfoodpills.com to bring the past future of technological marvels back into life. A long-term collector of digests, other paperbacks, mystery and science fiction and about 10,000 other books, he's writing a new history and bibliography of the seminal f&sf publisher Gnome Press (gnomepress.com). A collection of his own published science fiction, *Tyrannosaur Faire*, is available in paper and electronic format.

Follow The Digest Enthusiast on Pinterest for current releases and classic digest magazine covers in full color.
pinterest.com/richardkrauss/the-digest-enthusiast

Mystery, Detective, and Espionage Magazines by Michael L. Cook

Review by Richard Krauss

Admittedly, the number of reference volumes on my bookshelves is modest. Nonetheless, Michael L. Cook's *Mystery, Detective, and Espionage Magazines* is the most essential, complete and informative book on its topic that I've encountered. Its 1983 publishing date is its only real drawback. Until recently, most of the action in genre fiction magazines occurred on newsstands prior to 1983. But with the rise of self-publishing/online distribution, change is rapid and every year dates a reference volume like this one.

Cook explains in his Preface the why and wherefore of the book. Since escapist literature—mystery, detective and espionage in particular—is a preferred reading choice of the general public, Cook advocates it's an important resource to understand the attitudes and morals of the people who read it, within the context of the era in which it was published.

"There can be no claim made for completeness, although coverage of magazines published in the United States, England and Canada is fairly complete. Magazines included here are of both the professional and amateur categories, and nonfiction magazines providing commentary, as well as magazines providing fiction are included."

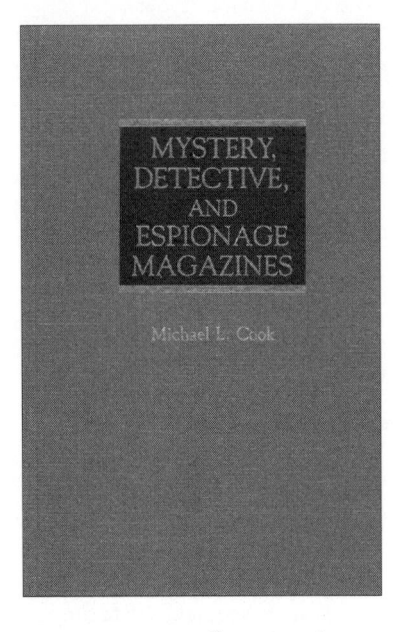

Defining the cutline for what's relevant and what's not, can be a source of controversy for researchers and collectors. Cook devotes a page and half to clarify his decisions.

Information on yesterday's popular culture has always been held in the hands of a few and not necessarily preserved through generations. In the pre-internet world it was often difficult to find authoritative resources and impossible to provide easy access to the information gathered. Few libraries valued and preserved this aspect of popular culture. Cook provides a list of the few who were building their collections in 1983.

A work of this size and scope can only be compiled with the assistance of many experts and contributors. Cook fills a page with his acknowledgements, many names familiar to collectors and avid crime fiction readers.

In the book's introduction, Cook provides a concise history of fiction magazines beginning with story papers and dime novels, then moving on to pulps and digest magazines. He touches briefly on key publishers, writers and characters and ends with an acknowledgement to fanzines. "Fanzines have made for themselves a significant place in the study, development, and enjoyment of popular fiction and are a vital part of it." No wonder a few, like *The Not So Private Eye*, are included in his listings.

The listings make up 627 pages, arranged alphabetically by magazine title. Each entry begins with a narrative summary of the title's significance, highlights of its run, a contents overview, key contributors and stories of particular note. Far too many fiction magazines saw only a handful of issues and Cook sometimes speculates on the reason a title ended such as poor funding, distribution, low quality, etc.

The wide-ranging sources of information gathered for each entry is noted, encompassing other reference volumes, private collectors, libraries, articles from magazines and fanzines, etc.

The publication history includes any title changes, number of issues, publisher, editors, original price, dimensions and page count, and current status—which for most is "discontinued."

The listings are comprehensive and I have seldom run across a title that is not represented.

As mentioned, the main section covers U.S., Canadian and UK titles, but it's followed by a section devoted to "Overviews of Foreign Magazines" that includes entries for Australia, Denmark, France, Norway and Sweden.

"Book Clubs in Profile" provides a rare look into the history of the book clubs that advertised in many of the magazines covered in the listings. Some like the Detective Book Club experienced amazing growth—from "the humble office in 1923 that rented for $480 a year" to a 23,000 square foot office on Long Island by 1954. Book clubs covered include Ellery Queen's Mystery, Masterpieces of Mystery Library, Mystery Guild (US and British), Mystery Library, Raven House Mysteries, Thriller (British) and Unicorn Mystery.

Appendices

A: Magazines by Category provides a quick reference to check formats. Separated into three groupings for the U.S., Great Britain and Canada, magazines are grouped as Dime Novels, Pulp Magazines or Digest Size Magazines. Further divisions separate fiction from nonfiction magazines.

B: Key Writers in the Golden Age "While this list is by no means complete, either for the authors listed or for the magazines in which they were published, it will serve to identify many of the early markets for these selected writers." A list of author pseudonyms follows.

C: Chronology provides the year in which each magazine originally appeared, beginning with 1882 (*New York Detective Library*) and ending with 1982 (*Hamilton T. Caine's Short Story Newsletter*, *Mystery News* and *Spiderweb*). Paging through the years it's easy to see when publishers felt most optimistic, and browsing the titles testifies how difficult it is to launch a title that lasts.

D: American True-Detective Magazines provides a partial list of magazines, noted "if for nothing more than identification, since many bear titles similar to fiction magazines." A list of 41 titles is certainly better than nothing, but I wish it were more exhaustive and included their size. None of the few pocket- or digest-size titles I've run across are included.

E: Canadian True-Detective Magazines

F: Sherlock Holmes Scion Society Periodicals "While some are of general interest to all who like Sherlock Holmes and Dr. Watson, others are primarily of value only to their own members."

G: Other Periodicals of Interest to the Collector Although its unlikely any of the 25 titles listed remain active, it may provide collectors new titles to seek out in secondary markets.

The final pages of Cook's volume include a two-page Selected Bibliography, Index and seven pages of Contributors.

Mystery, Detective, and Espionage Magazines
Greenwood Press, 1983
Hardcover, 6.25" x 9.5" 800+ pages
Prices ranges from $50 to $200 in secondary markets
Available at many libraries for reference

Art Taylor
Interview with the crime fiction writer.

Art Taylor is on a roll. An Agatha for best first novel: *On the Road with Del & Louise*; an Anthony finalist for both best first novel and best anthology, as editor of *Murder Under the Oaks*—so we're particularly grateful to him for making the time for this interview. Art's new-found recognition may be due to his novel and editing expertise, but he cut his teeth on short stories in digest magazines like *Needle*, *Barrelhouse*, and in large measure with *Ellery Queen Mystery Magazine*.

The Digest Enthusiast: As a youth, what stories first captured your imagination?

Art Taylor: I grew up in Richlands, North Carolina—a very small town, tobacco farms and hog farms—and a lot of the memories that stand out revolve around the woods behind our house: tromping through those woods with friends from our small neighborhood, cutting down small trees to build hide-outs, pursuing some kind of adventures, most of them driven by imagination as much as anything. Instead of being an alternative necessarily, reading served the same purpose: to open up the imagination to a wider world, to indulge that interest in adventure.

I've recently been going through some of my old books in order to introduce them to my own son, who's just turned four. Mostly it's just picture books that are appropriate for him now, of course, but looking through those, I was reminded how my parents had subscribed my brother and me to the Junior Literary Guild and the excitement I felt each time a new book arrived—whatever it was—and my mom

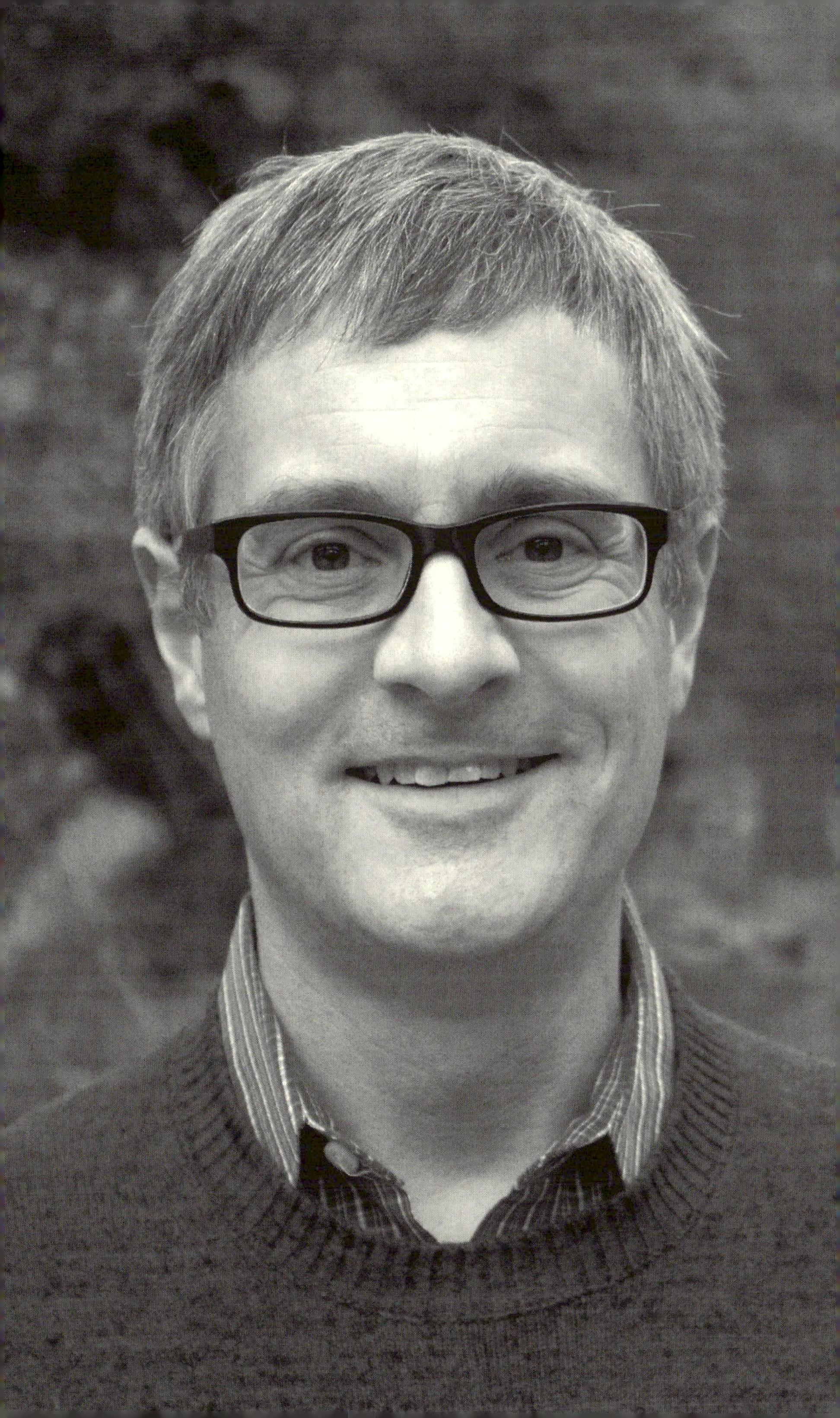

One Paycheck Away 2003 with Taylor's "The Blanketing Snow"

EQMM December 1995 Dept. of First Stories with Taylor's "Murder on the Orient Express"

reading *Tom Sawyer* aloud to me before I could read it myself. By the time I was actively choosing my own books, I'd gravitated toward mystery, suspense, and science fiction, and I've still got piles of them now: Encyclopedia Brown, Nancy Drew, the Three Investigators, Danny Dunn—and then pretty quickly those Choose Your Own Adventure books. (In fact, one of the Literary Guild books I remember best was a hardcover of Edward Packard's *Deadwood City*, one of the first of that series—even before it became a series.) When I transitioned toward adult fiction, mystery dominated again; John D. MacDonald's Travis McGee books and Harry Kemelman's Rabbi Small series each in their own way took me into other worlds, opened up the wider world.

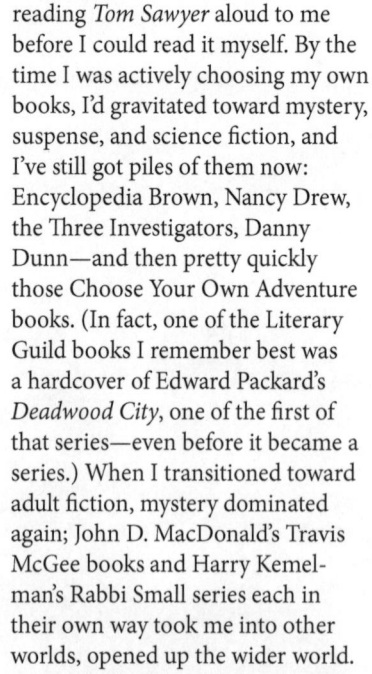

Somewhere late in elementary school, maybe early middle school, students were tasked with going door-to-door for magazine sales—a fundraiser for the school, of course. I can't remember what I sold, magazines to my parents I'd imagine, but I do remember subscribing myself to *Ellery Queen's Mystery Magazine*. I'd be hard pressed now to remember the first stories I read there, though Hugh Pentecost and Ed Hoch stand out as authors I looked forward to. That was really my introduction to the mystery short story—formative surely in ways I probably couldn't fully chart out.

TDE: When did the joy of reading lead to writing your own stories?

AT: I think the idea of writing always went hand in hand with my love of reading—that desire to create on the page for another reader the kind of experiences I was enjoying as a reader myself. Sometime in fall when I was in the third grade, I announced to my English teacher that I was going to finish my first book over Christmas break and she should look for it in the bookstore after New Year's; it was about a country mouse and a city mouse, as I recall. I remember a year or so later adding my pen name, Anthony Twig, to a novel I'd started; I'm sure it's in a box somewhere now, and I need to look for it one of these days. And then another night—what year I can hardly remember now—staying up late furiously working on an epic poem called "The War of Damascus"—writing lines, crossing out words, working and reworking, reading it aloud to see how it sounded, in love with the act of writing in a way I wish I still felt so consistently now. I do have that poem still on hand, just found it in the back of a filing cabinet; here's the opening stanza:

> *There once lived a man*
> *By the name of Belon,*
> *Who was swindled by*
> *A most masterful con . . . .*

I was always, always writing, but it wasn't until high school when I took my first formal creative writing course, with Grant Kornberg at Episcopal High School in Alexandria, VA. It was my first year at boarding school, and I'd submitted—very nervously—a short story to *Daemon*, the school's literary magazine. The story was called "Games" and it was heavily heavily influenced by Hemingway: a bar setting, two men talking about a woman, tight dialogue, a world-weariness that I surely hadn't earned myself. An hour or two after I tucked it into Mr. Kornberg's faculty mailbox, I heard him storming down the hall of our dorm, calling my name, telling me he loved the story, wanted to publish it, wanted to add me to his upper-class fiction workshop in the spring.

That was by far the best acceptance I've ever gotten (no editors literally knocking on my door these days!), and that course was the first I began thinking seriously of writing as a craft and not just a hobby.

Many years later, I found myself completing both an MA and an MFA in creative writing—the first from NC State and the second from George Mason University, where I'm still teaching now, and hopefully passing along the same kinds of tips and tactics and instilling the same level of enthusiasm that so many writers and professors have given to me.

TDE: When did you begin writing crime fiction?

AT: Here's what's funny (if that's the right word): Though mysteries were usually my favorite reads from childhood into my teen years, even at that young age I'd fallen prey to the idea that genre fiction was inferior to "literary" fiction. I mentioned Hemingway, for example, and so much of what I tried to write in high school and college was influenced in one way or another by what we were studying in the classroom: Flannery O'Connor and Eudora Welty and Raymond Carver or even Kafka or Pynchon briefly. Some of those did get published in some small literary magazines in my home state of North Carolina.

My first paid publication, however, was my first story in *Ellery Queen's Mystery Magazine*—"Murder on the Orient Express" (December 1995)—a story that wasn't originally intended as a mystery at all. Instead, it focusses on a couple honeymooning aboard the Orient Express and fumbling along a little from mishap to mishap, while the husband builds stories in his mind

EQMM June 2007 with Taylor's "An Internal Complaint""

about the other passengers—all of it imaginary, fueled by the spirit of Christie's novel of the same name. The story is about that imagination and how imagination suddenly helps the new marriage click, and—spoiler alert—ultimately there's no real crime in the story at all.

After that story was picked up for *EQMM*'s "Department of First Stories," I *did* try to write more traditional mysteries—an actual murder, a detective figure, a series of clues, etc.—but those fell flat one after another. It was only years later, over a decade actually, that *EQMM* took a second piece from me, "An Internal Complaint" (June 2007). This one too was in conversation with a classic text, Chekhov's "The Lady with the Dog," and here again too, it wasn't originally written as a crime story; in fact, the crime here was only unfolded in a very, very late revision. But this story was pivotal to me in terms of thinking of my own writing, the fiction I wanted to write—focused on relationships, on questions of responsibility and often on moments of betrayal, but also driven by what always drew me to crime fiction: plot-driven drama, suspenseful pacing, and crime as an event that can reveal some truth about a character, either reveal it to other characters or to the reader or even as an epiphany to the characters themselves.

TDE: What led you to teaching?

AT: Teaching has become a rewarding career in many ways, but I'd never actually planned on it. When I came to George Mason University to pursue my MFA, I was fortunate to earn a teaching assistantship—working first in the university's Writing Center and then moving into the classroom. (The phrase "teaching assistant" isn't really accurate in this case, since I wasn't anyone's assistant, but simply headed up the courses myself.) The position came with tuition waiver—a tremendous benefit—and then a surprise: I actually enjoyed it and was apparently good at it, since the English Department asked me to stay on as a professor after I'd completed my degree.

My courses range widely—from composition courses (for business students, actually) to literature classes that focus on some aspect of crime fiction or true crime and then to creative writing workshops in both fiction and nonfiction. Those latter classes have been the ones where I've learned the most, in two directions. First, trying to lead discussions on a subject, whether it's surveying the history of detective fiction or talking through approaches to crafting short fiction,

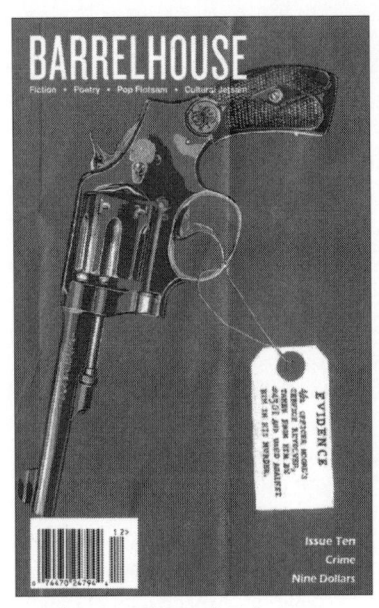

Barrelhouse #10 2011 with Taylor's "Blue Plate Special"

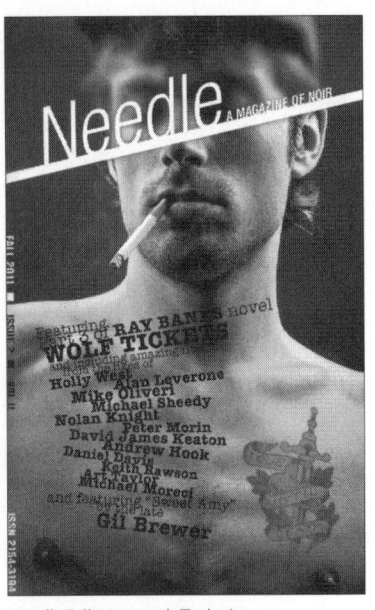

Needle Fall 2011 with Taylor's "The White Rose of Memphis"

has helped me to understand and to articulate my own thoughts on those subjects in ways that might otherwise have been more amorphous or even nebulous. Second, whatever I've offered the students, I've also learned something from them and from their fresh perspectives on topics. It never fails in a workshop setting, for example, that someone in the class sees something in a submission that I missed or offers constructive criticism in directions that I hadn't anticipated.

Always in the classroom, my approach is less about lecturing, less about telling, and more about listening or about following—about all of us on a journey together, all of us hopefully discovering something new along the way.

TDE: Between teaching, conventions, and everything else, when you do find time to write?

AT: Ideally, I try to make writing part of my everyday routine; in reality, it's unfortunately not always the case. Writing in the morning, first thing before diving into emails and the other "pulls" on the day, often proves the most productive for me, since my mind is sharper, less cluttered, and if not more focussed necessarily, at least more open to imaginative thinking. But particularly during the school year—when I'm juggling lesson plans, heavy reading loads, and then piles of grading—writing first thing in the morning isn't always an option and often it gets pushed to the back burner or the next day . . . or the next or . . . .

I do, however, believe that at least touching base with a project each day keeps that imagination firing even when I'm not actively sitting in front of the computer working. Many of my writer friends try to meet a quota—either a time quota (certain number of hours

EQMM August 2009 with Taylor's "A Voice From the Past"

writing each day) or a word quota—but more productive to me is the idea of consistency, whether that means jotting down a single note or writing a full scene or whatever. Each of those is a step forward, and even a single step forward is better than standing still.

TDE: You're juggling a lot! How do your stories evolve—do you make an outline or start with a vague idea and just dive in?

AT: Different stories evolve in different ways and often over very different periods of time. Maybe the quickest story I ever wrote was "Mastering the Art of French Cooking" for *PANK*'s crime issue. I was at a concert with my wife—the band *Chicago* or what's left of it these days—and it turned out to be kind-of boring (my wife's the fan, not me), so my mind started to wander. By the end of the concert, I'd pretty much sketched out the story in my head—it's structured around a recipe for Coq au Vin—and the next morning I spent a couple of hours actually writing it, then had my wife read it, then spent another hour revising it. I emailed it to the editor around noon and by early afternoon I'd gotten an acceptance—so one of the quickest stories not just in terms of writing but also in terms of acceptance.

At the other end of the spectrum, I wrote about half of my story "A Voice from the Past" and then put it aside for several years, not sure where to go next with it. When I returned to it with fresh eyes, I came up with ideas about the rest of the plot, what seemed suddenly not just right but maybe inevitable, given all the seeds I'd planted in the first half.

Generally, I spend a lot of time thinking on a story—sketching it out in my head, at least big chunks of it—before I begin writing at all. Often what's sketched out isn't necessarily the beginning; sometimes it's a big chunk of the middle or maybe the ending. But once I do start writing, structure is a primary focus: the arrangement and movement of scenes, those building blocks toward the larger architecture of a story, getting them all to fit right, balance properly, hold one another up.

That's definitely a slow process sometimes, despite that one story I mentioned. Even when I think I've got a lot of the character, the plot, the structure worked out, the writing itself is inevitably a process of discovery for me—reading as much as writing, figuring out what's there and bringing it all out.

Some of what I'm about to say may sound a little . . . eccentric? I don't know the word. But I do tell my students, often, that they need to listen to their stories-in-

EQMM May 2011 with Taylor's "A Drowning at Snow's Cut"

EQMM Mar/Apr 2013 with Taylor's "The Care and Feeding of Houseplants"

progress and that by listening properly, they'll learn what the story needs. And I try to do just that with my own work too.

TDE: Your stories often include a particular interest or experience like sailing, houseplants, prep school, etc. What influences these choices? Do you draw mostly on existing knowledge or research?

AT: Some of my fiction draws on my own background and experiences. "Rearview Mirror"—the opening of *On the Road with Del & Louise*—was inspired by a trip my wife and I took to New Mexico several years ago. Similarly, "A Drowning at Snow's Cut" was based in part on a boat trip my father and I took down the North Carolina coast. "A Voice from the Past" centers on some hazing incidents very similar to the rat system at the boarding school I attended. All those are pretty heavily fictionalized beyond those core elements, of course, but building from that foundation has helped to fuel the imagination.

For "The Care and Feeding of Houseplants," however, I was in new territory. I know little about plants, and they regularly perish under my own care. But plants—and plants versus animals—seemed a necessary metaphorical element to the story I was working on, so I ended up reaching out to a botany professor here at George Mason University with some questions.

Funny story there—partly a plot spoiler, I'm afraid. When I emailed her—this was back in 2007 or so, as I recall—I also asked about ricin, and she quickly responded that I should call instead of emailing. When I did get her on the phone, she told me that she'd worked at Quantico for a while and that our email exchange had probably already been flagged by the government because of that mention of ricin. I laughed at the time.

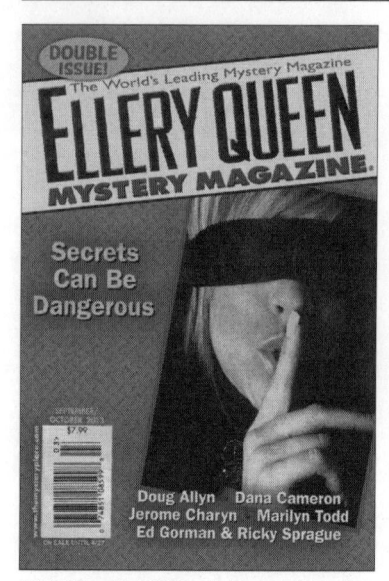

EQMM Sep/Oct 2013 with Taylor's "Ithica"

Seriously? Like the government is checking through everyone's emails? Again, this was around 2007, so . . . .

TDE: Most of your stories are character driven. You explore relationships, reactions and decisions that characters have to live with. What appeals to you about this approach?

AT: Basically, I think those themes are just at the core of my own interests and obsessions. A fellow writer, E.A. Aymar, pointed out to me—nicely—that I wasn't very good at branding my work, since my stories were all over the place in terms of subgenre and tone and whatever: noir here, cozy there; traditional structure here, something more experimental there; etc. And I'm certain that readers who have enjoyed some of my darker stories might well be bewildered by some of the lighter comedy of *On the Road with Del & Louise*. But to me, so many of these stories come down to the same elements: the responsibilities inherent in being in a relationship; the times when that relationship is tested; the decision to respect or betray the relationship; the fallout from that decision. Whatever the circumstances or situation that might drive that central storyline, and whatever the various combinations of choices and consequences that might result, those questions and that theme are what I return to time and time again.

TDE: What things have most helped you grow as a writer?

AT: Several things. First, I would not be where I am in terms of craft without the workshop structure, by which I don't necessarily mean having gone through the MA or MFA programs that I attended, though that's where I first experienced such workshops. Nothing that I write gets submitted for publication without having earned some feedback from several writer-friends. Their responses and suggestions provide perspectives that I wouldn't be able to gain myself no matter how long I worked on a story. I've learned and grown as a result of those conversations.

Second, and maybe related, I'd point to the larger literary community. We always think of writing as a solitary art, but the support and encouragement of groups like Mystery Writers of America and Sisters in Crime has been invaluable, and that's true of any of the other communities I'm fortunate to be part of. All of us are cheering one another on, reading one another's work, celebrating successes, offering support during tough times—reminding one another that it's all worth it.

Finally, specifically, I would need to credit Janet Hutchings at

This Job is Murder 2012 with Taylor's "When Duty Calls"

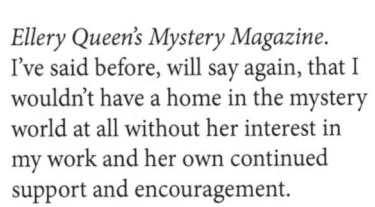

EQMM Nov 2014 with Taylor's "The Odds Are Against Us"

Ellery Queen's Mystery Magazine. I've said before, will say again, that I wouldn't have a home in the mystery world at all without her interest in my work and her own continued support and encouragement.

Beyond that, in terms of advice to other writers, I'd fall back on that same mantra: read, read, read, read, read. All of us learn from and grow from immersion in what's come before.

TDE: Your novel, *On the Road with Del & Louise*, is earning awards and praise with crime fiction groups and readers. How did your work with the editor at Henery Press help in its development?

AT: I was very fortunate with the support and guidance I received from the folks at Henery Press. *On the Road* wouldn't be the book that it is—wouldn't be a book at all, in fact—without that support.

At the point at which Kendel Lynn approached me about the possibility of working with them, I didn't have a manuscript to submit—but I had completed a second story with Del and Louise, and I outlined to Kendel some ideas I had for other stories, all contributing toward a longer story, an overall narrative arc, for the characters. I submitted those first two stories and then some extensive plans for the full book to her, and pretty soon we had a timeline for me to finish the full book. Once I'd submitted that final manuscript, the editorial letter I received back from Kendel and from Rachel Jackson had a number of suggestions for restructuring, rewriting, increasing dramatic tension, adding, subtracting, etc. that overall made individual stories sharper and then strengthened the overall novel, bringing it all together.

TDE: The book is described as "a novel in stories." I can't help but think of some of the great television series today, when I hear that phrase. Why write a novel in stories?

AT: I've struggled before with writing more traditionally structured novels; there are a couple of failed manuscripts I could point to on that. So the novel in stories provided me the opportunity to build on what I have indeed been able to write—short stories—and put them into service as building blocks toward that larger structure. And I've been pleased to hear from most readers that the components here do ultimately cohere as a novel, just as I'd hoped and planned. There's a storyline that threads through the individual adventures—those interweaving and overarching narrative arcs—and other elements are designed to pull it together: resolutions to individual stories that then find twists in later stories, or motifs and imagery that recur but also shift from appearance to appearance.

I didn't consciously think of TV series as a model when I was writing the book. However, in retrospect, I think that's likely one of the easiest ways to explain the structure—and certainly my own TV watching over many, many years has likely inevitably informed my understanding of dramatic structure anyway. A full season of a TV show needs to have a continuing narrative arc, but a single episode should also have a full beginning, middle, and end. This is a more recent show (well, recent is relative, I know), but Veronica Mars works so nicely here: each episode a single case, but various clues and plot points along the way leading toward a larger investigation that doesn't find resolution until the final episode of the season—at which point you look back and see all of it with a clearer perspective. That's different from something like Columbo (another favorite!) where each episode stands alone and there's nothing threading the episodes together.

TDE: You edited *Murder Under the Oaks*, the Bouchercon Anthology 2015. What was it like editing the work of other writers?

AT: Being on the other side of the desk proved to be a real joy overall. We had over 170 blind submissions, as I recall, but after the first round of readers went through them, only 27 were passed my way for consideration—which I needed to cut down to a dozen that would go along with the stories from the invited contributors (primarily guests of honor at that year's Bouchercon). While maybe any of those stories might well have worked for the anthology, my guiding principle in selecting the final ones was the need for diversity, really in keeping with the range of writers and writing that you'd find at Bouchercon itself. Crime fiction covers a lot of territory, of course—from cozy to noir and with a lot of other subgenres in-between, for example, and I know how often readers have faulted mystery anthologies for not having enough detective-driven stories. So I wanted a mix of light and dark, a mix of contemporary and historical, a mix of protagonists from detective figures to victims to criminals. I hope the final line-up provided a little something for all readers.

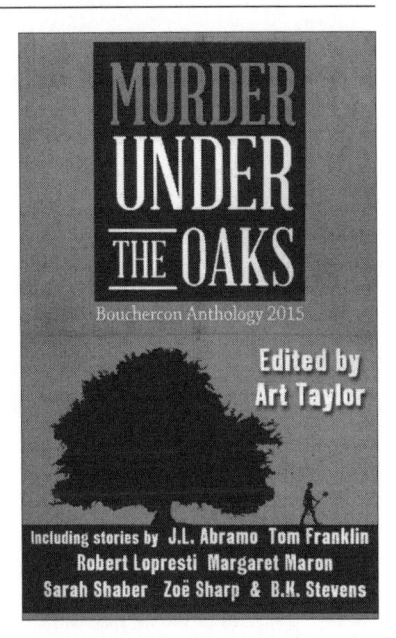

In terms of actual editing, my goal was to help each writer guide his or her story toward the highest fulfillment of its own potential—if that's the best way of saying what I'm trying to say. I always want to avoid trying to get a writer to revise according to how I would write the story, but echoing what I said earlier about "listening" to stories, I felt in a couple of cases that writers weren't following up fully on some of the elements they'd introduced into their own stories or that the balance of their storytelling was off somehow, and I tried to help guide them toward a better balance or toward fully engaging with those aspects of the story that they'd left underserved. A couple of stories in particular come to mind on this, and in each case, I tried to explain my concerns and then let the writer address, rather than me just, say, stepping in and trying to rewrite myself—which would seem like overstepping boundaries. In each case, those writers not only responded beautifully within the stories themselves but also seemed very grateful for the feedback, which made me feel like maybe I did my job there OK.

In any case, it was a pleasure to help pull the anthology together, and it's tremendously gratifying to help champion other writers' work and particularly to bring first-time writers into the limelight—much more fun to promote someone else's writing than to try to promote your own!

TDE: Ha! But how do you promote your own work? What was your most effective promotional activity or strategy?

AT: "Effective" may be a stronger word than I can address properly here, I have to admit! As most writers know, the business and marketing side of the process may well be more challenging than the craft side of it. I spend a lot of time on social media (is there a better procrastination tool?), especially Facebook, and I've built some great friendships there with writers and readers, some of whom I've never even met in person before. I've gained a lot from those relationships, in terms of thinking about craft or of being inspired and encouraged, and it's been a pleasure to follow many of those writers' careers as they've grown or to share news of books and stories with fellow readers and book lovers—so much to learn from them. Just recently, for example, Kathy Harig of the bookstore Mystery Loves Company offered a couple of things online. First, she shared news about local writer Karen Huston Karydes' *Hard-Boiled Anxiety*, a Freudian study of Hammett, Chandler and Macdonald, and I ended up booking Karydes to speak at our local MWA chapter and now her book is on my desk—can't wait to dive into it. And later, Kathy posted a question on Facebook about everyone's favorite novels and stories by Daphne du Maurier, a short but fun conversation amongst her friends (a partial overlap with my friends) which ultimately added both to my reading list and in the process to my thoughts about du Maurier and her appeal.

Having written all that, I need to come back to the original question, I know. I'm not sure how often any of those interactions with friends, fellow writers, and fellow readers ever prompts someone to check out my own work, but I also think there might be something troubling with keeping that concern (is my social media promotion working?) too much at the forefront of any conversation. The engagement is the pleasure first and foremost, the friendship and connection itself the primary goal. Any promotional value is just bonus beyond that.

TDE: Looking ahead, do you plan more series or stand-alone stories? Shorts or novels?

AT: I've got several ideas for book-length works—a couple of them also with a novel-in-stories structure. Most recently I've been working on a trio of interconnected novellas about a reclusive bookstore owner and a spunky young accountant in a Nero Wolfe/Archie Goodwin kind of relationship. And then, building off the boarding school story we talked about earlier, I've been considering a longer work in a similar setting—one which has always struck me as perfect for tension and suspense and danger. That one too might be constructed in some fragmentary way: a mosaic of pieces that would be part crime story, part coming-of-age tale, part reflection. But as I've been considering the projects, several folks with better perspectives on the industry (better than I have) have told me that such projects are tough sells to readers—and to publishers as well—and that a more traditionally structured novel might be a better move. I love the short story, and I'll keep writing them, of course, but in terms of book-length works, I guess I'm still feeling my way.

TDE: What are you working on right now?

AT: At this very moment, I'm finishing up a short story for the anthology *Coast to Coast: Private Eyes from Sea to Shining Sea*—my first turn at a private eye tale—and then there are a couple of stories whose drafts I'd like to revisit, stories which never quite seemed to come together but which stand out for me as having potential. Each of them are ambitious, more so than some previous stories in terms of scope and structure, and they've therefore been more of a challenge. One of them, in fact, I've worked on for several years, first as a short story, then at novella length, then as one strand of a multi-layered novel manuscript (one of the failures I mentioned before), and now back at novella-length—adding, developing, trimming, reshaping.... Ultimately, I hope to get that one right.

TDE: What are the best ways for readers to keep up with you?

AT: I try to keep my website at www.arttaylorwriter.com updated as regularly as possible, including a blog section to which readers can subscribe. Following up on my comments before, you can also find my Facebook author page by searching for "Art Taylor, Writer" or find me on Twitter at ArtTaylorWriter, and I keep those updated not just with my news but also with news I find interesting or informative, and those social media accounts are good ways to stay in touch generally. I appreciate the friendship and conversation, and hope to see folks there!

TDE: Thanks for sharing your thoughts, Art. It's been a great pleasure learning more about you and your work.

AT: Thank you again for thinking of me here. This has been very much fun!

Galaxy Magabook No. 1 by Lester Del Rey, cover by Virgil Finlay

The Galaxy Magabooks
Article by Gary Lovisi

"WANTED: Vigorous man, with training and experience in scientific exploration, to undertake dangerous and unusual assignment. Apply in person, this evening, 6 to 10. Dr. Hilaire Crosno, Hotel Crichton."
Excerpt from *After Worlds End* by Jack Williamson

Galaxy Books were an outgrowth of *Galaxy* magazine, where science fiction stories originally published in the digest magazine were reprinted as paperback books for the emerging 1950s SF fan and collector market. I'm not going to go into all the books in the series in this short article, but a bit of history is in order.

Galaxy Books began in September, 1950 with a run of 31 digest-size paperbacks. In 1958, the last four books in the series (#32–35) were published as regular short-size paperbacks. In 1959, Beacon Books continued the series with 12 tall-size paperbacks that ran until 1961. All are very collectable. [See Steve Carper's article on page 62.]

This brings us to 1963 and the Galaxy Magabooks. By this time the format had evolved and gone full circle. The Galaxy Books series began in digest-size, then became paperbacks of various sizes, and finally ended here as digests. The series, at least in format, had ended in the same format in which it had begun. The Magabooks are a little known digest-size addendum to Galaxy Books, but are a nice little set of digests in their own right.

I always wondered about the name of these books. For a long time I thought of them, and subconsciously called them "Megabooks", perhaps assuming that because each book combined two novels in one book, that "mega" was a natural name for them. But it wasn't. When I looked at the books more closely I saw that they're called Magabooks, which seemed odd to me; and for a bit I wondered about that name. What did it mean? I soon realized that it was a kind of amalgam for "magazine book" and that since *Galaxy* magazine, and the Galaxy Books both originally began as digest-size magazines—the name fit well.

The three Galaxy Magabooks are all from 1963 and all are first editions—thus, the first time such novels were combined in book form. They feature some of the better 1950s pulp science fiction by three masters of the genre: Lester Del Rey, Jack Williamson and Theodore Sturgeon. The books proclaim "Two Complete Novels" by each of these three authors—with two covers—of a type. This was perhaps inspired by the Ace Doubles, but before Ace there were SF and mystery pulps that used very similar cover designs when combining two books into one issue. Later Belmont Doubles and even Lancer 2-in-1 Books used a somewhat similar format, showing two titles and two covers for a combined edition. The Galaxy Magabooks did not have a uniform cover art design, but they did have a uniform titling format. However, each book had a different cover artist, with art done in different styles, and in different format designs. It was a series that apparently never really found its proper place and was probably doomed to failure.

The first two books: the Del Rey and Williamson feature more pulpy stories and cover art. By book

Galaxy Magabook No. 2 by Jack Williamson, cover by Ed Emshwiller

#3, written by Sturgeon, the series seems to be making an attempt to leave the pulpy image behind with more adult material and design. Unfortunately this was the last book in the series. I would have loved there to be many more books in this series. Book #3 is also, for some reason, difficult to find.

Listed below are the Galaxy Magabook digests along with the back cover blurbs that tell a bit about each of the stories.

No. 1: The Sky is Falling & Badge of Infamy
by Lester Del Rey, 1963, cover art by Virgil Finlay

Badge of Infamy: "He was one of old Earth's outcasts, driven to share the wretched life of the Martian colonies—with nothing to live for, and only a dream, to die for!"

The Sky is Falling: "Wizards of far-future science, they

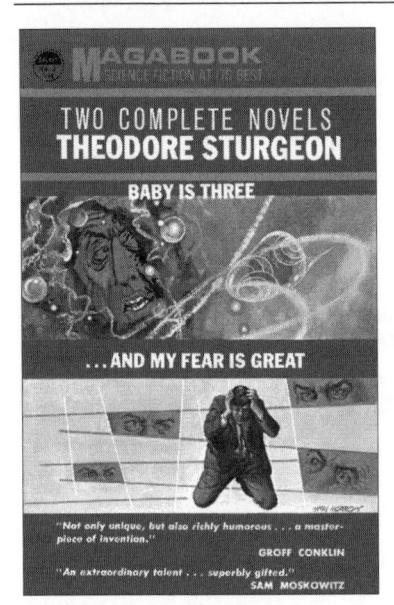

Galaxy Magabook No. 3 by Theodore Sturgeon, cover by Gray Morrow

snatched him from the jaws of death into a fantastic life drama and danger at the end of time!"

No. 2: After Worlds End & The Legon of Time
by Jack Williamson, 1963, cover art by Ed Emshwiller

After Worlds End: "In this strange world danger was his every day companion—despair dogged his steps—and the greatest peril of all was his only hope for life!"

The Legion of Time: "They stormed the wall of the future on the trail of one woman who was too evil to live—and another who might never be born at all!"

No. 3: Baby is Three & . . . And My Fear is Great
by Theodore Sturgeon, 1963, cover art by Gray Morrow

Baby is Three: "The boy went to the psychiatrist because he needed help—but his problem was something no analyst could handle. He knew his name—but not his identity. He knew what he did—but not what he was. Worst of all, he didn't know how many of him there were."

. . . And My Fear is Great: "The fear that lurked inside him was a demon that drove him to desperate measures of hatred and terror. It promised him all the riches of the earth. It carried him to a God-like power—until it met an even more frightful monster outside!"

The back cover blurbs, while perhaps doing their job to whet the appetite of the browsing bookstall buyer as to what lay inside the books, really do not tell much about the stories themselves. I've not read them in many years, but remember them all as good, solid science fiction, and I have always been a fan of Williamson's Legion books, and the two Del Rey adventure novels. No Galaxy Books collection can be complete without this last gasp, off-beat and rather idiosyncratic science fiction series. *Enjoy!*

"The Science Fair is two blocks down."

Criswell Predicts: Fate & Spaceway

Article by Tom Brinkmann

"'Criswell Predicts' and everybody listens. For many years Criswell has been hailed as the 20th Century Nostradamus and is the first prophet to gain prominence and national recognition since Edward Bellamy and his 'Looking Backward.' Criswell has become a household word and is the most quoted personality of our time."

The Great, Legendary, & Amazing Criswell

Jeron Criswell Konig ("King" in German), aka Charles Criswell King, aka Jeron Criswell King, aka Jeron King Criswell (his most used), aka "Jack Paar's Seer," aka "The 20th Century Nostradmus," aka "The Great Criswell," aka "The Legendary Criswell," aka "The Amazing Criswell," (August 18, 1907–October 4, 1982) was born in Princeton, Indiana.

These days, Criswell's biggest claim to fame were his roles in three of Ed Wood, Jr.'s cult movies: *Plan 9 From Outer Space* (1956, originally titled, *Graverobbers From Outer Space*), *Night of the Ghouls* (1959, released in 1984, after both Wood and Criswell had died, by Wade Wellman who paid Wood's unpaid processing bill), and his most lengthy role in *Orgy of the Dead* (1965).

Criswell, Vampira (Maila Nurmi), and Tor Johnson had their resurgence of fame in the 1980s largely due to an interest in Ed Wood, Jr. that culminated with Rudolph Grey's research and book *Nightmare of Ecstasy: The Life and Art of Edward D. Wood, Jr.* (1992) which is credited with sparking the interest in Tim Burton to make his film *Ed*

An Accurate Glimpse of the Future
CRISWELL PREDICTS

Criswell's column "logo" first appeared in *Fate* #18 March 1951 and was later used in his columns for *Spaceway*.

Wood (1994) in which Criswell was well played by actor Jeffrey Jones.

But, Criswell began his career long before he met Ed Wood. In 1939, after having moved to New York City, Jeron Criswell co-authored and self-published four "how-to" books with his future wife, Louise Howard (the two were married from 1940–74). Their books were titled; *How Your Play Can Crash Broadway*, *How To Crash Tin-Pan Alley: The Authoritative Handbook For A Successful Songwriting Career*, *How to Crash Broadway*, and *You Can Have It . . . Anything You Want*. Interestingly, those books had ads in the back for two additional books, *Evasive Joy*, a novel by Louise Howard, also self-published by Howard & Criswell, and *The Game of Life and How To Play It* by Florence Scovel Shinn (1871–1940) which had been published in 1925. Shinn was at first an illustrator who later became a "spiritual teacher and metaphysical writer" and was a proponent of the "New Thought" movement. Shinn's teaching and philosophy on life were evident in a later book, *Success Without Struggle*, which Jeron King Criswell wrote in Hollywood and published in 1950.

Louise Howard was actually the pen name of Myrtle Louise Stonesifer (1905–1985), aka Halo Meadows, a stage name she chose for her stint in burlesque theatre. These two "eccentric" people found themselves in New York City in the 1930s, she hailing from Littlestown, Pennsylvania.

While in New York City, Jeron King Criswell and Louise Howard at first pursued theatrical careers and were in a stage production together, with Arthur Jones their composer, of Oscar Wilde's "Life and Loves of Dorian Gray." Criswell later had a small part in Mae West's Broadway show, *Catherine Was Great* (1944/45) which went on tour but, only lasted nine months.

In Rudolph Grey's seminal book on Ed Wood, *Nightmare of Ecstasy*, Maila Nurmi, aka "Vampira," stated she had met Criswell in Los Angeles at the Ranch Market while getting a chili dog. Nurmi had just finished her show at KHJ, which was across the street, and "was in full [Vampira] drag" at the time. Criswell, recognizing her, said, "Oh, my, you're, you're Vampira, you're Miss Vampira. I have a friend who would love to meet you. She'd be so delighted. I'm referring to Miss West, Mae West . . ." Nurmi, who had also been in West's Broadway

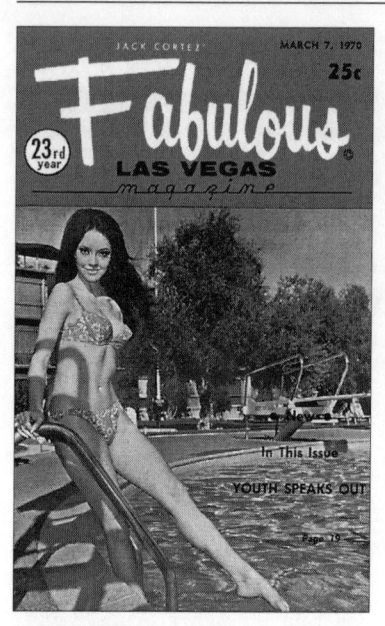

Jack Cortez' *Fabulous Las Vegas* March 7, 1970

production *Catherine Was Great* in the 1940s, was puzzled, and asked, "She would be delighted to meet *me*?" Criswell answered in the affirmative, saying, "She's a great fan of yours." Nurmi then informed him, "Well, she's already met me, she fired me from *Catherine the Great* [sic]." Thus, Criswell became the "go between" for Nurmi and West.

Nurmi went on to add, "[Ms West] loved to cook, and when she thought she'd done something really nice, she'd send it over in her limousine with her chauffeur to Criswell. And then he'd call me up, 'cause I was starving, and he'd say, 'Miss West sent us some Swedish meatballs.' So I'd go over and we'd eat them."

Eventually, Criswell landed a radio broadcasting job that led to his filling lag-time with his predictions which became popular. Thus, "Criswell Predicts" was born. He started writing columns in the *New York Enquirer* in the early 1950s where he had two columns, printed on the same page; one titled, "Jeron King Predicts," and the other, "The Answers To Your Problems," in which Criswell answered readers' letters. In June 1957 the *New York Enquirer* became nationally distributed and became the *National Enquirer*. The *Enquirer* then changed the title of the column to "Thru CRISWELL'S Eyes YOU See the FUTURE." Criswell had become a syndicated columnist in 300 to 1,000 papers, depending on whose figure you choose to believe.

His "Criswell Predicts" column had a long run in two tabloids published in Chicago, the *National Informer* and its sister tabloid *Rampage* from 1962 until late 1971. And, the short-lived *National Free Press* (1965–67) in which his column was titled "Predictions by The Great Criswell—Jack Paar's Seer." All three papers were published by The Informer Publishing Co., Inc.

Criswell and his wife Halo moved to Los Angeles, California where he had his own fifteen minute TV show, *Criswell Predicts*, on Los Angeles's KLAC in 1953–57 and went on to appear as a guest on numerous radio and TV shows from 1959–70, namely, *The Jack Paar Program*, *The Jack Paar Tonight Show*, *The Tonight Show Starring Johnny Carson*, and *The Mike Douglas Show*. Criswell would occasionally tour America with his predictions as a monologist, playing theatres and auditoriums. Most of Criswell's predictions were wild and zany and most did not come to pass, although, the few that did boosted his popularity. On *The Jack Paar Program* of March

Seven Seventy Publishers' *Hippies Vol. 1 #4* 1967

10, 1963, Criswell is said to have predicted "... that President Kennedy will not run for re-election in 1964, because of something that will happen to him in November 1963."

Criswell and his columns could be found in everything from the national tabloid newspapers to scandal and entertainment magazines from the 1950s through the early 1980s. Some of the publications he could be found in, besides *Spaceway* and *Fate*, were Jack Cortez' Fabulous Las Vegas Magazine (1960s–early 1970s), the tabloid/magazine *Modern People* (1977), and even *Buy-Lines Press* (1980), to name a few.

One of the more curious, funny, and rare appearances of Criswell in print was a 1967 "adult slick" magazine titled *Hippies* published by Seven Seventy Publishers. The cover of the magazine has both "Criswell Predicts Bottomless" and a film still of a bearded Titus Moody staring up from a boat at the bikini-clad bottom of a woman walking along a dock. You might wonder, "What was Criswell doing in a magazine about hippies?" The answer is Criswell was friends with Titus Moody, another fringe Hollywood personality. Moody took many photos of the various youth cultures happening around Hollywood and the San Fernando Valley in the 1960s, such as Love-Ins, Be-Ins, outlaw bikers, hippies, and the Sunset Strip Riot. These he sold to certain publishers of the adult slicks, and packaged magazines for them, mainly Seven Seventy Publishers. Moody most likely took the photos of Criswell posing with topless and bottomless females that appeared in the eleven-page feature, "Criswell Predicts Bottomless," and probably packaged the magazine which also contained photos of hippies taken by Moody.

The *Daily Mail* newspaper, published in Anderson, South Carolina, published the "Criswell Predicts" column from 1954–1971. The paper's owner also owned Droke House books which published Criswell's three books of predictions titled, *Criswell Predicts From Now Till the Year 2000!* (1968); *Criswell Predicts Your Next Ten Years* (1969); and *Criswell's Forbidden Predictions Based on Nostradamus and the Tarot* (1972). Interestingly, Droke House also published a diverse assortment of other authors and subjects such as: *The Quotable Billy Graham* (1966), *The Quotable Richard M. Nixon* (1967), *"Hear Me Out: This Is Where I Stand"* by George C. Wallace (1968), and *A Flash of Swallows* which consisted of poems by Steve Allen writing as "William Christopher Stevens" (1969).

In 1970, Criswell released a spoken word LP on Horoscope Records titled *The Legendary Criswell Predicts Your Incredible Future* which is now a collector's item but, was reissued on CD in 1998 by Mad Deadly Worldwide Communist Gangster Computer God.

Fate: True Stories of the Strange and the Unknown

When I originally started this article it was only to be on Criswell in *Spaceway* magazine but, while doing reaserch on Criswell, I was reminded when I did a search on eBay, that there had been an article on him in *Filmfax* magazine (#110) back in 2006. I knew I had that issue, somewhere, in my vast labyrinthine collection of magazines and located it. I had read the article ten years ago but had forgotten that I had. As it turned out, I saw in the article, "Criswell Predicts: The Life and Prophecies of the Amazing Criswell," by Edwin L. Canfield, that it had come from his yet to be published biography on Criswell. So, I searched for the book only to find it had never been published. I then searched for the author to find out what had happened to the book. When I made contact with him I learned it was basically done but he had let it sit for a while. But, in our email exchange I also learned that Criswell had written four articles in early issues of *Fate* magazine, which I did not have.

Ultimately, I found three of them on eBay but, thanks to publisher/editor Richard Krauss who had two of them, including the one I didn't find, he kindly and promptly sent me PDF files of the two articles he had so I could start writing about them.

For the most part, these early predictions of Criswell's were concerned with the social, political, financial, and generally more mundane aspects of post-WWII America and the world. In other words, they were less incredulous than his later predictions from the 1950s and 1960s, and therefore were more problematic to write about. As Criswell once told a friend, "[I] had the gift [of prophecy], but . . . lost it when I started taking money for it."

Fate Vol. 1 #4 Winter 1949

The "Criswell Predicts" radio broadcast had preceded his writing of articles and columns and Criswell's "87% correct" claim had been established by the time Ray Palmer wrote his editorial in this early issue of *Fate*. Palmer, writing as "Robert N. Webster," seemed most concerned with the accuracy of Criswell's predictions and stated, "We're going to 'keep score' on him and see whether or not he can live up to his reputation for correctness. Incidentally, Mr. Criswell will appear in FATE each month with predictions for the coming month, or with special prognostications that may apply." Criswell did not appear monthly as Palmer initially stated; he actually only wrote in the four issues listed here.

"Criswell Predicts For 1949!" by Jeron King Criswell was obviously written at the end of 1948 and he started by posing questions to the reader, such as, "Will the Federal Government continue to hand out money—or is the bonanza of the war years at an end? Will we have socialized medicine? Will there be federally controlled radio like the

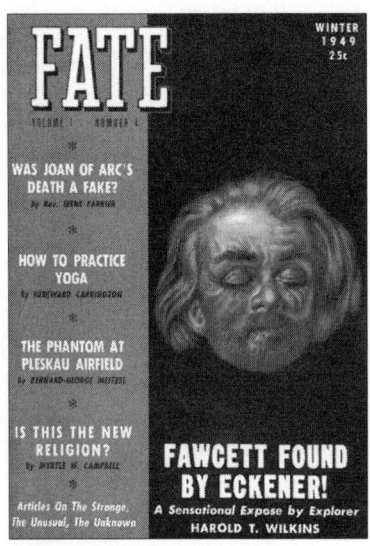

Fate Vol. 1 #4 Winter 1949

British Broadcasting Co.?" Then, Criswell related a strange prediction he claimed was made by Leonardo da Vinci in 1445: "In 500 years, man shall make an instrument, shall drop it from the sky from a man-made bird, it will stun the earth and cause all to drop dead from its very breath, shall devastate buildings and entire cities—with its pink umbrella of a cloud." Then, Criswell pointed out that 1445 + 500 = 1945; after which he leapt into his first prediction, that the atomic bomb would be dropped somewhere in Asia by late Spring of 1949.

Criswell seems to predict the self-regulated Comics Code Authority of 1954:

"There will be a tight federal censorship control over motion pictures and the subjects shown on your local screen. Comic books will be made more suitable for children."

And, color TV which was sold in 1954 for the first time; although I'm not aware of any color programs that could have been shown on it:

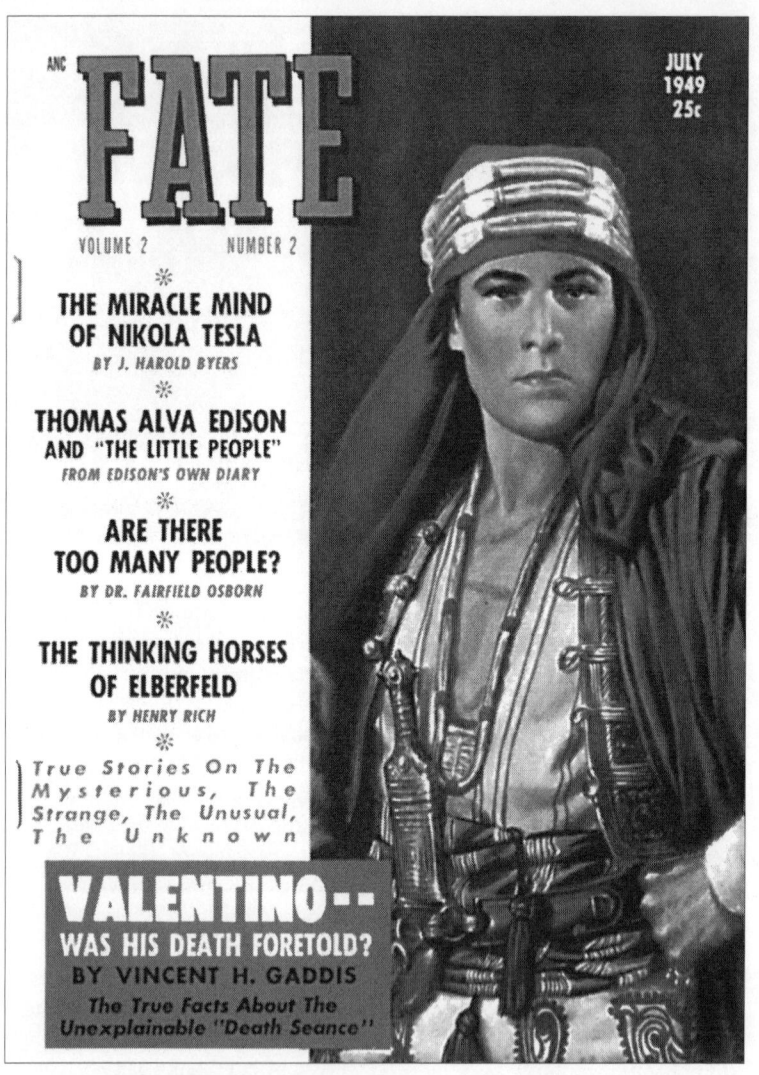

Fate Vol. 2 #2 (issue #6) July 1949

"Radio will be cleaned of all phoney contests, ism-messages and programs not considered good taste. The news out of 1949 is that you will be able to enjoy television in your home on a $50 set—or rent one at the price of $5 a month, the cost of your telephone rental! There will be television in natural color by 1950!"

Criswell then predicted on "the international scene" for several pages, which included predictions for most of the countries in Europe, and a few other specific countries such as Turkey, Russia, Japan, Mexico, and general predictions for the continents of Africa, Asia, and South America.

Criswell also claimed he felt Hitler was still alive and ". . . will be heard from in 1949!" And, gave his reader's a barrage of inventions to come in 1949, which included:

"... *a pen that writes with perfumed ink ... ladies hats with propellers in the crown like Junior's ... a machine that will give you a sun-tan in one minute ... a new drug that will make you fat, and a newer one that will slim you down ... pink aspirins for children, and mint flavored ones for adults ... a box of black stationary with white ink ...*"

And so on.

Fate Vol. 2 #2 (issue #6) July 1949

On the first page of this second "Criswell Predicts" article, *Fate* listed twenty predictions that Criswell had made in the Winter 1949 issue that had come to pass in the month of January 1949; Ray Palmer keeping his promise to his readers that he would "keep score" on Criswell's correctness.

Criswell had kept a diary writing down predictions he received from other seers, writing:

"*Twenty years ago this month, an Arab, who read the future of the world in coffee grounds outside a cafe in Fez, Morocco, told me '1929 will be a year of money crisis, 1939 a year of war crisis, and 1949 a year of personal crisis!'*"

Then, Criswell quoted Napoleon, who said, "You cannot dispute a prophet, you can only disbelieve him." After that, Criswell started by answering six questions "... that confront the American people on this 25th day of January, 1949."

The last four-plus pages of the article were taken up by Criswell predicting on "people, places and things," of which I give you the following samples:

"*The Men of the South still have

Fate Vol. 4 #2 (issue #18) March 1951

the power of filibuster, and will use it, if any civil rights below their sacred Mason-Dixon are tampered with. This filibuster will be loud and long at the end of the congressional session; nevertheless, the negro will have his vote—not in 1949 but in 1950.*

"*The latest Mexican food import will be pickled rattlesnakes with wild crickets. Peru's bid for the epicure is baby mountain crow stuffed with mint leaves and puya. (Puya is bug juice.)*"

Fate Vol. 4 #2 (issue #18) March 1951

The "An Accurate Glimpse of the Future: Criswell Predicts" logo was used in this issue; the same logo was used eventually in the *Spaceway* digests. At the start of this article was a boxed-in comment that read:

"*For over 10 years, Jeron King Criswell, the Indiana Prophet, has peered into the future. His forecasts have been 87 per cent accurate. His syndicated column appears in 44 daily newspapers; his transcribed radio program over many stations, and his television appearances bring an avalanche of mail. During the single month of June, 1950, Criswell received 830,000 fan letters. At present he is on a lecture tour of 30 states. Here are his predictions for the year 1951. Read them and judge for yourself. See end of article for special offer to FATE readers."

The offer was to send in a self-addressed stamped envelope to *Fate* "to receive a personal prediction from Criswell."

In this article Criswell predicted, "1951 will be the connecting link of two 50-year periods, which make up our 20th century. This conjuction will be fraught with fire, fear and trembling!" This sounds more like the 21st century's "Culture of Fear" since 9/11/01 to me. Criswell's family had a long history in the funeral business and he made many predictions having to do with it, like the following:

"Competition will become so great amoung the funeral directors of the nation, because of the longevity of you people who are not dying fast enough, plus more and more funeral parlors opening up, that a price war will ensue. You will read of 'Funerals for Only $50' ... 'Let us see you to the pearly gates for only $35' ... and other slogans in this new cut-rate trend. Funeral Directors, like doctors, fear the oncoming socialization of their art."

And:

"By 1952 we will have a strong movement for Federal cremation. It will be pointed out that we are using up valuable land for burial grounds, and are also polluting our water systems by present burial customs."

Two of Criswell's other favorite subjects of prediction were nudism and the superiorty of women. As for the later, he predicted:

"Women will come into their own this coming year. In 1952, it is my prediction that the Republicans will nominate a woman for vice president to run with Eisenhower ... and that this will be the fusion ticket that will win! The woman is Mrs. Margaret Chase Smith from Maine."

Fate Vol. 6 #4 (issue #37) April 1953

In the article, "Prophecies I Have Heard" by Jeron King Criswell, there is a photo of him with a note from the editor (not named) next to it that explained the article as Criswell revealing tales from a diary he had kept through the years containing all the many "soothsayers" he had consulted going back to his childhood, and the accuracy of their predictions. Throughout the course of the article Criswell tells of predictions he had received by means of a "palmist," a lady who could talk to the dead (i.e., necromancer), a spread of playing cards, "the embers of a dying fire," dreams, tea leaves, "a sand-diviner," a crystal ball, and astrology from Sydney Omarr, "the astrologer's astrologer."

Starting as a boy with a gypsy palm reader, or "palmist," to whom he gave his hard-earned fifty-cents and was told, "You will leave here when you are 16 and not be the doctor you plan to be." As Criswell related, "I had planned to follow the footsteps of a great-uncle but when I did leave home at 17 to attend the university I changed my mind completely about being a doctor." You may wonder, as I do,

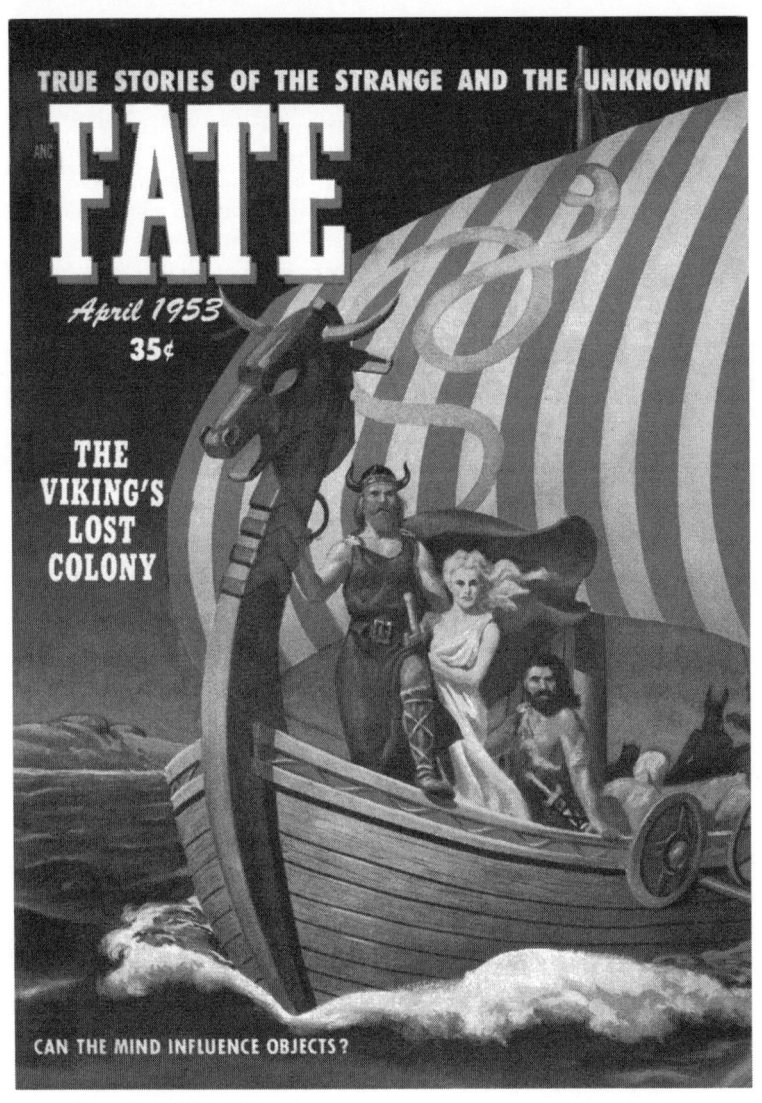

Fate Vol. 6 #4 (issue #37) April 1953

was it the gypsy's prediction that came true, or Criswell's memory of it that helped it come true?

Some of the more interesting prophecies Criswell recalled:

"... *a nameless tea-leaf reader in a Gypsy Tearoom at 43rd and Fifth Avenue, New York, told me I would spend the following year in Europe. This too strangely came to pass."*

It is interesting that the address given for the Gypsy Tearoom was one block south of the address given for Howard & Criswell, publisher of their 1939 books, which I assume was where the two were living at the time.

And, while visiting Europe, Criswell must have made a side-trip, as the next predic-

Fantasy Book Vol. 1 #5 1949

tion he wrote about said:

"*In Casablanca, Morocco, a sand-diviner predicted that my voice would be heard over the air selling coffee! This happened 20 years later and I consider it most remarkable.*"

And, the weirdest:

"*A fortune-teller in Marseilles foretold a great disaster which I would witness upon returning to America. I was within 50 feet of the Graf Zeppelin when it exploded.*" [Strangely he didn't name the Hindenburg that exploded on May 6, 1937 in New Jersey, but I assume that is what he was talking about.]

Criswell ended the article recalling:

"*Only a short time ago Rev. Beulah Englund, 1900 West Sixth Street, Los Angeles, called me on the telephone and told me I would be asked to write an article for a national magazine within the next week. This article is proof of her prediction!*"

In his book, *The Life and Curious Death of Marilyn Monroe*, Robert F. Slatzer, a Hollywood journalist who was a friend of Monroe's for sixteen years, included a chapter titled, "Psychics, Seers, Psalms and Palms," in which he wrote:

"*Marilyn also reminded me of the time I introduced her to my friend Jeron K. Criswell ... We were having lunch at the Brown Derby back in 1950 when I saw Criswell waving to me from across the bar. He joined us for a drink, and when Marilyn found out who he was, she inundated the gray-maned Criswell with a barrage of questions.*"

"I was really impressed by his truthfulness," Marilyn recalled. "And his prediction about me came true."

At the time (1950), Monroe had been in less than ten films, all bit-parts, most notably *Love Happy*, *The Asphalt Jungle*, and *All About Eve*. Criswell had told Marilyn, "You're getting a late start, but you'll finish ahead of all the others. I predict you will become not only a successful actress but the most famous blonde in the world."

The rest of the chapter in Slatzer's book told of Marilyn's fascination with visiting fortune-tellers, which leads me to wonder whether Criswell might have regaled her with some of the same experiences he wrote about in this article for *Fate*.

Spaceway: Stories of the Future/Science Fiction

The word "spaceway" is an odd word by its very definition: "A route used for travel or shipping in outer space." And, the digest, *Spaceway: Stories of the Future*, was a unique publication. William L. Crawford (1911–1984) was its editor and publisher with his imprint Fantasy Publishing Company, Inc. Crawford had been sporadically publishing science fiction fanzines since 1934 when he published the two titles *Marvel Tales* two issues (1934/35) and *Unusual Stories* two issues (1934/35) as Fantasy Publications. In 1947 Crawford started *Fantasy Book*, publishing six issues, through 1951. *Fantasy Book* contained stories by such sci-fi/fantasy luminaries as A. E. van Vogt, Frederik Pohl, Forrest J. Ackerman, L. Ron Hubbard, Andre Norton, Charles Beaumont, and Robert Bloch. Interestingly, in the later issues of *Fantasy Book* was a poetry feature titled, "Songs of the Spaceways," which was edited by Lilith Lorraine.

But, Crawford's biggest claim to fame was publishing the first and only book by H. P. Lovecraft published in Lovecraft's lifetime, *The Shadow Over Innsmouth* (Visionary Publishing Company, 1936). The book had a dust jacket and interior illustrations by (my personal favorite Lovecraft illustrator) Frank Utpatel but, it also contained so many typos that Lovecraft "insisted on an errata sheet (which also was faulty)."

Next, came *Spaceway: Stories of the Future* launched in 1953. *Spaceways* was the title of a 1953 UK movie directed by Terence Fischer that starred the US actor Howard Duff, as well as Eva Bartok, Alan Wheatley, and others. It had been a radio play written by Charles Eric Maine which was then turned into a screenplay by Paul Tabori and Richard H. Landau. *Spaceways* was released in the US in August 1953 and the UK in late December of that year. *Spaceway: Stories of the Future*'s premiere issue was also dated December 1953 and contained "A Novelette by the

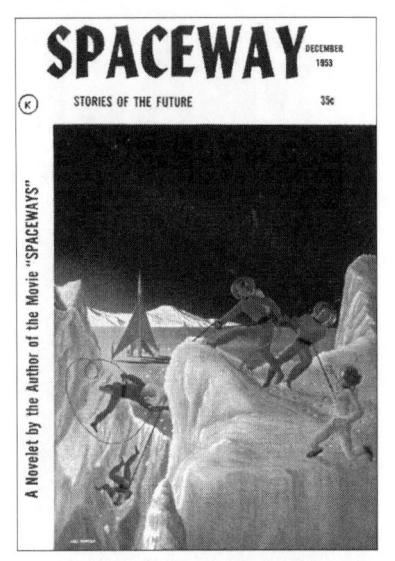

Spaceway Vol. 1 #1 December 1953

Author of the Movie 'Spaceways,'" i.e., Charles Eric Maine, which was titled "Spaceways To Venus."

Spaceway First Run:

Vol. 1 #1 December 1953, 164 pgs 35¢
Mel Hunter, cover art. Contributing writers included: Charles Eric Maine.

Vol. 1 #2 February 1954, 164 pgs 35¢
Mel Hunter, cover art. Contributing writers included: L. Ron Hubbard and Forrest J. Ackerman.

Vol. 1 #3 April 1954, 164 pgs 35¢
Mel Hunter, cover art. Contributing writers included: H. J. Campbell, August Derleth, and Forrest J. Ackerman.

Vol. 2 #1 June 1954, 132 pgs 35¢
Paul Blaisdell, cover art. Contributing writers included: A. E. van Vogt and Forrest J. Ackerman.

Vol. 2 #2 December 1954, 132 pgs 35¢
Paul Blaisdell, cover art. Contributing writers included: Charles Eric Maine and Forrest J. Ackerman.

Vol. 2 #3 February 1955, 132 pgs 35¢
Paul Blaisdell, cover art. Contributing writers included: George H. Smith, A. E. van Vogt, and Forrest J. Ackerman.

Spaceway Science Fiction Vol. 2 #3 February 1955

"An Accurate Glimpse of the Future Criswell Predicts: On Outer Space," kicked off the issue, which contained one illustration by cover artist Paul Blaisdell, and was prefaced by the following note:

"'Criswell Predicts' and everybody listens. For many years Criswell has been hailed as the 20th Century Nostradamus and is the first prophet to gain prominence and national recognition since Edward Bellamy and his 'Looking Backward.' Criswell has become a household word and is the most quoted personality of our time. You may read Criswell's syndicated column in over 1,000 newspapers. You may view him on your television set, or hear him on your radio. Criswell holds the attendance record in many theatres and auditoriums throughout the country. We consider SPACEWAY most fortunate in securing Criswell's exclusive predictions on Outer Space. The Editors"

The piece opened with Criswell's famous line, "We are all interested in the future, for that is where you and I are going to spend the rest of our lives." Then, Criswell continued on with his profound observation, writing, "Outer space can be an inch away from the end of your nose or six trillion miles. I predict that the following will be a short history of man's future—in outer space . . ." Criswell predicted the extent of man's future in outer space as building a space station and reaching the moon, both of which have come to pass, then there was to be an "all-out war," "a 20th Century Armageddon" which "will leave the earth a radioactive ruin." But, there would be survivors. Criswell then predicted that the survivors would work overtime to build "a huge cube in outer space, which will be ten miles in height, ten miles in width, and ten miles in depth." There is mention of "an electric brain the size of a thimble" that choses the brightest and best scientific, medical, and moral people to man the cube into outer space. This is the cube or, "nation in the sky," that Criswell is seen gazing upon on the cover.

The one flaw was what the "all-knowing, analytical, mechanical" brain controling the cube didn't know—"the philosophy and psychology of the female brain." Hence, the revolution by the females led by the "Joan of Arc of outer space," who was a product of artificially inseminated breeding in the laboratories of the cube. The women bring about this revolution by building two generators that will send a massive electrical shock to the controling brain which fuses its wires together rendering it useless. Then, Criswell predicted: "The men will revolt against this change of conditions, but the women triumph for they will have the power to build a consciousness that cannot be turned by outside interference."

Meanwhile, the earth becomes a distant memory for the space-cube-nation and disappears "as a spark vanishes in a bonfire, and its charred remains will drift somewhere in the vast regions of time as a cinder floats on the wind . . ." Criswell could write a damn good descriptive sentence.

Criswell ends his piece with these amazing, hilarious, and somewhat incredulous, predictions:

"I predict there will be only four things remembered out of the 20th Century—four things they can definitely prove existed. These four things will be a mechanical eggbeater, the music of Liberace, Mae West, and someone by the name of Eisenhower who seemed to accomplish so very much for humanity.

"A copy of this Spaceway Magazine will be treated with a special preservative in the hopes that this future generation may find these predictions startlingly correct."

At the end of Criswell's article, there was an italicized sentence that read, *"For the benefit of those that wish to know more about Criswell, we are reviewing on the following pages his forthcoming picture CRISWELL PREDICTS TO 1999."* The curious review on the next page was titled, "Panic On Celluloid," by Charles F. Wireman, which was most likely Criswell himself using a pseudonym.

Spaceway Science Fiction Vol. 3 #1 April 1955

Wireman claimed to have seen celebrities "milling around" the entrance of a screening room at "a major sound studio in Hollywood" and was intrigued, so he mixed in with the crowd as they entered. When the title *Criswell Predicts To 1999* appeared on the screen, in color, Wireman wrote, "I immediately thought it was simply another futuristic science-fiction movie, but soon found out this was DIFFERENT!" Wireman also claimed the musical accompaniment was "rather strange and intriguing" and the film narration by Criswell "will hypnotize anyone." Criswell is one of two writers I can think of whose voice you hear in your head as you read their writing, the other being William Burroughs.

The film, according to Wireman, consisted of sequences, "in vivid color," of various "strange and horrifying events" that were to befall Earth in the years leading up to 1999. Disasters such as: "a tremendous stratic explosion will cause the entire world to be without lights for 40 nights and 40 days," "a widespread type of leporacy," "a terrible human carnage," and "devastating fires, the explosions of diridgibles, nudism [a favorite Criswell prediction], great sea monsters, dying planets, and the sinking of a continent." Just the nudism combined with leporacy, in vivid color, would be horrifying enough! Luckily, Wireman mentions an intermission which gave him, and the rest of the audience, time to catch their collective breath.

Wrapping up the review, Wireman gave these details, "[The] film was produced by George Richter and Wayne Berk, with a musical score by Scott Seely. Running time is presently 90 minutes. There are some overlong sequences which will evidently be trimmed before the actual release." I could find no mention of this film existing anywhere and both Rudolph Grey and Edwin Canfield confirmed its non-existence, which is too bad as it sounded like a winner to me!

Vol. 3 #1 April 1955, 132 pgs 35¢
Paul Blaisdell cover art. Noted contributing writers: Jack Lewis, Forrest J. Ackerman, and Criswell.

"Criswell Predicts: The Dying Planet," in which Criswell informed his reading public of the future death of the planet Bellarion and the coming consequences for planet Earth. Bellarion, an inhabited planet similar to our own, but in another solar system, was leaving its orbit and would eventually "shoot off into the depths of space" to its destruction. Criswell warns his fellow earthlings, "We shrug our shoulders at the fate of Bellarion because we feel it does not concern us, nor will it influence our life—but there is where we are wrong!"

Bellarion's scientists sent out an interplanetary S.O.S. which was received by "an international Disaster Commitee" on earth. Then, Criswell stated, "learned experts are working twenty-four hours a day studying the reports they have received." The people of Earth learn that Bellarion is "headed upon a course which will eventually bring it into our solar system." And, according to Criswell's prediction, that's when the cosmic poop hit the fan and, it got really weird, really fast.

As Bellarion sped through space and closed in on our solar system, there was "a strange feeling of tenseness in the air" on earth. Once the errant planet entered our solar system and was seen crossing our skies, all manner of craziness ensued. As Criswell predicted:

"The human body itself will become an individual chamber of torture. Human heads will swell to twice their size, due to the blood rushing to topmost extremities. Pregnant women will explode."

And...

"In cemeteries, the dead will be lifted from their graves through a strange magnetic force which will influence only dead cells. Cadavers will mingle with the living, floating about aimlessly."

Many other catastrophes to befall our planet were predicted—dormant volcanoes will erupt, buildings will fly into space, the courses of rivers will change, South Dakota will become a lake, floods, fire in the sky, and so on. There was a Paul Blaisdell drawing included to illustrate the madness.

The final horror comes when, "The skies will rain blood because of the millions of crushed bodies floating in space." When the bloody rain stops, Bellarion explodes, raining hot ashes down on earth that spark fires which "will sweep nation after nation, leaving only smoking ruin."

Miraculously, some humans survive all the biblical shenanagins of Mother Nature and hold "a great memorial service for all those dead on this planet and other planets, including the millions of Bellarion." Then, "the restoration of Earth will be undertaken." Criswell believes the planet is to endure a cycle of cosmic disasters, writing, "Cleansed hearts, strong hands and a loving spirit will be our only tools to build for the next cosmic disaster." And, in the next to last paragraph, Criswell challenges the reader:

"I predict this will one day happen in what we call the Future. Can you prove that it will not? If you have scientific proof to offer, I would be most happy to examine it."

Another short article by Charles Wireman followed, titled, "Jeron King Criswell," which was a short biography (or autobiography, as the case may be) that gave some "intimate facts" on Criswell's life. Starting with his methods of prediction *"... by careful analysis, with an almost supernatural sense in reading the stock market charts and graphs, sifting the daily newspapers for obscure items that will have propelling results at a later date, talking to specialists in their own fields for information on the latest trend, always seeking inside tips which will cast a shadow of a coming event. Through trend, precedent, pattern of habits, and the unalterable laws of cycle and human behavior..."*

Not surprisingly, you learn that Criswell's favorite American author

Spaceway Science Fiction Vol. 3 #2 June 1955

was Edgar Allen Poe. Then, Wireman wrote that Criswell's "most cherished newspaper interview was with the late H. C. Wells," which at first I thought was a typo. But, following that Wireman wrote, "Criswell considers H. B. Wells' 'Things To Come' one of the most remarkable books of the 20th Century, for its astute insight into the future." For starters, I'm not aware that Criswell ever did an interview with H. G. Wells, and doubt he did, and that might explain the first "typo." The second fudging of Wells' initials is slightly more perplexing. Wells' book being titled, *The Shape of Things To Come* (1933) which was shortened to *Things To Come* for the 1936 film made from it.

More intimate facts were revealed: "Criswell comes from... one of the oldest funeral families in America," he attended Cincinnati University for one year, and did "editorial and newspaper work in New York." Criswell's dietary likes were, "rare meat, buttermilk, peanut butter, raw tomatoes, apples and dark bread."

And, the piece ended saying, "Criswell's next project, besides his coast-to-coast television show, will be when he takes his one-man auditorium show into the Hollywood Bowl on August 18, 1955 [Criswell's 48th birthday]."

Vol. 3 #2 June 1955, 132 pgs 35¢
Paul Blaisdell, cover art. Noted contributing writers: George H. Smith, Ralph Milne Farley, Forrest J. Ackerman and Criswell/Mae West.

This June 1955 issue of *Spaceway* may have been the first time Criswell and Mae West (August 17, 1893–November 22, 1980) shared a cover together but, it wasn't the last. The *National Informer*'s July 1, 1962 issue (volume 1, #6) used a photo of them together on its cover and was the first issue of the *Informer* that carried Criswell's column. The photo was probably taken in the mid-1940s when Criswell had a small role in West's stage production *Catherine Was Great*. That was the photo which artist Paul Blaisdell (1927–1983) used to paint the *Spaceway* cover, to which he added the spacesuits. The caption under the *Informer*'s cover photo read:

"*The Great Criswell, who makes predictions for the readers of* The National Informer *Newspapers, Jack Paar, and NBC-TV's* Tonight Shows, *also gives hints about the future to beautiful Mae West, the*

Criswell and Mae West from the cover of the *National Informer* July 1, 1962

everlasting star of the movies. Miss West may now read her future in The Great Criswell's columns in The National Informer *Newspapers.*"

I don't think Ms. West needed to read the *Informer* for her predictions of the future, as Criswell was her personal psychic and they had remained friends since *Catherine Was Great*. West even wrote and recorded a tribute song titled, "Criswell Predicts," which can be found on her 1956 LP *The Fabulous Mae West* (Decca). Criswell attended West's funeral in 1980 in a wheelchair as he had suffered a couple of strokes in the late seventies.

"Criswell Predicts: On First Moon Flight," is the final and wackiest of his three articles for *Spaceway*. It is also where Criswell engaged in some heavy-duty name dropping. Criswell started by stating, "These words are being written in 1965, for we have projected ourselves into the future." Then, he asked the reader to think back to the violent "Battle of the Ballots" presidential election of 1960, where men and women fought in the streets over a male candidate and a female candidate. The women, and their candidate, Miss Mae West, won. Making Mae West the first woman president of the United States!

The first thing President West did was make good on her main campaign promise, to get Congress to grant her the funds "for the first Rocket Express to the moon." The rocket would be built by Boeing in Witchita, Kansas and tested at the Sand Flats near Las Vegas for "Flight—Destination Moon!"

Then, the article took a weird turn as Criswell veered off into a "quote" from the Sunday, May 9th, 1965, *New York Enquirer*. I guess Criswell couldn't predict that the paper had turned into the *National Enquirer* in June of 1957. And, the quoted article was written by none other than "the international correspondent Charles Wireman."

Before Criswell started the quote, he dropped a heaping load of twelve names on the reader. These were the journalists, gossip columnists, radio commentators, and so on, that were to cover the launch and return of "the greatest event of the 20th Century," the first moon flight; included were Walter Winchell, Lowell Thomas, Hedda Hopper, Dorothy Kilgallen, Edna Ferber, Louella Parsons, and Sheila Graham, to name a few.

Wireman/Criswell started the *New York Enquirer* "article" by giving the rocket launch details; the rocket was one thousand feet long, it had been named "American Lunar I," and the launch was being broadcast 24-hours worldwide. The members of the moon expedition were many but, the most notable were: President Mae West and Criswell, "her specially appointed space diplomat," as well as others that included aide, George Liberace.

President West "was attired in a form-fitting, smartly-tailored space suit, which had an unnatural gleam in the sun, like a glowing flame." President West said nothing as her "bubble-like" space-helmet was attached. Then, putting her fingers to her helmet, over her lips, blew the assembled crowd a kiss and waved goodbye. She entered the rocket followed by Criswell and the rest of the lunar expedition. Then the door to the rocket made a "clank" as it shut behind them. Then, the rocket was launched as the crowd fell silent—destination, moon.

"People kneeled unashamedly on the streets; traffic stopped by itself; trains, busses, and planes interrupted their schedules; all labor stopped abruptly, for this was truly the most wonderous moment since Eternity began!"

Thus, the *New York Enquirer* "article" ended. Lastly, was an "official statement" that President West released on the expedition's return to Earth that started with a feminist quip, "Fear has never been in the vocabulary of a woman, and it was up to a woman to accept the challenge of space flight! But I was very disappointed with the Moon!" President West's disappointment seemed to be the discovery of no inhabitants or animal life and the ground being "spongy." But, they did discover "some traces of a very strange vegetation."

On the positive side, President West announced that plans were being made to colonize using airtight buildings; ground work was being laid to make the Moon the fifty-first state in the U.S.; and the declaration of May 9th as a national holiday named "Lunar Day." To sum up the expedition President West claimed, "If we of the 20th Century have done nothing more than to open the Gateway to the Moon, we have done much!"

Criswell ended the piece by writing:

"My friend, we are most fortunate to be alive in this magical year of 1965, for it is truly the pivotal year in the History of the World, and will rank in importance with the year 1492!"

Spaceway Second Run

Vol. 4 #1 January 1969, 132 pgs 50¢
Morris Scott Dollens cover art. Contributing writers included: E. C. Tubb, Ralph Milne Farley, and A. E. van Vogt.

Vol. 4 #2 June 1969, 132 pgs 50¢
Morris Scott Dollens cover art. Contributing writers included: L. Ron Hubbard and Forrest J. Ackerman.

October 1969, 132 pgs 50¢
Morris Scott Dollens cover art. Contributing writers included: Andre Norton, Robert E. Howard, and Forrest J. Ackerman.

June 1970, 132 pages 50¢
Morris Scott Dollens cover art. Contributing writers included: Andre Norton and Emil Petaja.

Bibliography

Canfield, Edwin L. "Criswell Predicts: The Life and Prophecies of the Amazing Criswell," *Filmfax Plus* #110, April–June 2006.
Grey, Rudolph. *Nightmare of Ecstasy: The Life and Art of Edward D. Wood, Jr.* Los Angeles, CA: Feral House, 1992.
Howard, Louise and Jeron Criswell. *How Your Play Can Crash Broadway: The Authoritative Handbook For A Successful Play-Writing Career.* New York, NY: Howard & Criswell, 1939.
Jones, Arthur (as told by), Louise Howard and Jeron Criswell. *How To Crash Tin-Pan Alley: The Authoritative Handbook For A Successful Songwriting Career.* New York, NY: Howard & Criswell, 1939.
Slatzer, Robert F. *The Life and Curious Death of Marilyn Monroe.* New York, NY: Pinnacle House, 1974.

Highly Recommended

Criswell's forthcoming biography *Forbidden Predictions: The Life and Prophecies of the Amazing Criswell* by Edwin L. Canfield.

Acknowledgements

Edwin L. Canfield for cluing me in to Criswell's articles for *Fate* and answering my questions.
Rudolph Grey for sharing his files on Criswell and Titus Moody.
Richard Krauss for his encouragement and sending the PDF files.
Kathleen Banks Nutter for cheerleading, line editing, and borrowing the 1939 Howard & Criswell books from the Neilson Library, Smith College.

Tom Brinkmann writes about unusual, off-the-beaten-path magazines, digests, and tabloids at his website: badmags.com His books *Bad Mags* volumes 1 and 2 are available from amazon.com. Grab one or the pair and you'll be off and running into the land of twilight pulp and the glossy adult hinterland!

Brinkmann started writing reviews of zines and books, and articles on weird magazines for *Headpress Journal* (UK) in 1998. His Bad Mags site has been on the Internet since 2004; *Bad Mags* V1 was published in 2008, followed by *Bad Mags* V2 in 2009. Since then he continues his pursuit of printed matter of unusual interest in his self-published zine *On the Rack*, of which there have been three issues. To get your copies, which are in limited supply, contact him at: vaioduct@aol.com

Strangers in Need

Science fiction by Joe Wehrle, Jr

He stood looming above her, his not unhandsome face shielded by a strange curved transparent plate, the rest of his body sheathed in a rubbery material that seemed like a second skin, rife with strange contrivances.

The snow-covered hut stood alone, a tiny, silent bastion against the thoughtless winter's cruelty, its smoke billowing up against the sombre gray sky. Through a chink in the wall, a small girl's eyes gazed out at the icy stillness.

The wind had died down and the snow lay in silent, drifted expanses amid the trees, unmarked by prints of man or beast. Shoving a piece of wood into the hole, Ariadne turned from the austere scene and stood watching her sleeping parents. They had been ailing for a number of days, her father rising only long enough to go out in search of some hapless fowl or a collection of edible roots to sustain them, then sinking back on his rude bed of wood and skins before he had eaten his full share. Her mother usually prepared the food, and might sit listlessly in company with her daughter after they had eaten, but before long she, too, would fall into a restless sleep, trusting Ariadne to keep the fire burning.

The time of Winter Festival was drawing near, and as yet the girl had nothing to give her sick parents. The very fact of their illness sharpened her anxiety about the lack of a special present, for she felt that if she could only gift them with something truly wonderful, happiness alone might make them well. Her father had once told of a man who found a great precious jewel, just lying in the forest, lost there by traveling nobility. Thinking thus, she fed a few more pieces of dry wood to the fire, and then, bundling up tightly in her rough furs, went out into the winter morning to see what she could find.

At the sound of her feet crushing through the fresh snow, a rag-tag, battered-looking dog emerged from its sheltered den, quietly favoring the game leg to which it had grown accustomed. Silently it followed her through the trees and over the drifts, until they could no longer have been seen from the yard of the hut.

Ariadne tucked her pale, braided hair deeper into the folds of the fur hood and looked around. There was a stark, unchanging appearance to the forest, whichever way she turned. Her footprints in the snow, and those of the dog were the only indication of the way back. Even the spacing of the trees seemed everywhere the same.

Against this monotonous background, the strange footprints she came upon clashed, shocking her senses when she came upon them. The thing that frightened her most was the size of the prints. They looked like the impressions of a grown man's feet, but could any man grow so huge? She remembered her father's stories of the frost giants who constantly did battle with the gods. Legend foretold that ultimately the frost giants would persevere and destroy the world. Terrified, Ariadne turned to run, and almost blundered into the maker of the footprints.

He stood looming above her, his not unhandsome face shielded by a strange curved transparent plate, the rest of his body sheathed in a rubbery material that seemed like a second skin, rife with strange contrivances. The dog barked, and Ariadne, paralyzed with fear, screamed shrilly into the icy air.

She had thought the giant man was moving forward to seize her, but Ariadne suddenly realized that he was falling instead. His huge body toppled forward and to one side of her, heavily landing face down in the snow. He lay unmoving for a moment as the girl stared openmouthed and the dog circled warily, then he roused and lifted himself on one elbow. Ariadne noticed now that his leg was injured; the rubbery covering was slashed below the knee, and blood stained the snow beneath that leg.

The large man brushed snow from his faceplate and regarded her thoughtfully. His hand beckoned her closer, the gesture only serving to send her several halting steps in the opposite direction. The dog, however, edged forward hesitantly, and the giant nodded and made further reassuring gestures until the sorry beast's head moved near enough for him to stroke with his oddly-gloved hand. The eyes behind the glazed shield met Ariadne's again, and she smiled charmingly and came forward.

It took all his waning strength and all of Ariadne's efforts to get the giant standing again. He clung to the trunk of a small tree with one arm and swung the other over a low branch for leverage while the girl shoved at his good leg until it was in a straightened position. He hung on, the dog at his side, while she searched for a sturdy fallen branch to serve as a staff. The new-fallen snow made looking difficult, but she finally spotted one lying across a notched limb and went running back with it.

In his weakness, the stranger needed her support as well as that of the staff. He took a few tentative steps and shook his head violently when Ariadne pointed in the direction of her home. Easing one hand off the staff, he indicated a direction to their right. Puzzled, the girl nevertheless did as he wished. The dog ran ahead, prancing excitedly on his three good legs.

It was not a long trek, but it proved a difficult one. Though the staff bore most of his weight, Ariadne was soon gasping with the effort of keeping the weakened giant from falling sideways. As they wandered into deeper forest, she looked back anxiously at her tracks, but the frozen land still lay calm, and the way back was clearly marked.

Over a low ridge they struggled, Ariadne's eyes continuously scanning the ground for pitfalls, her tired arms constantly steadying the large man's faltering steps. Only when they reached the bottom did she look up and see the strange silvery vessel resting on the forest floor amid the trees it had broken in its descent. The huge stranger smiled down at her tiredly, and pressed two fingers to his belt. Ariadne watched as the heavy metal doors slowly rolled aside, then she moved forward to the portal with the injured giant, the dog following hesitantly.

Inside, a moving metal path carried them through one chamber into another and came to a halt. Ariadne swayed drunkenly and the giant fell wearily into a chair that seemingly grew from the metal floor, yet spun around at his touch.

He removed his helmet and dropped it to the metal plating with a crash. A tool he produced quickly separated the rubbery armor at the knee, and he gingerly pulled the lower section off.

His great hand moved to the wall beside the chair, and he pressed one of the tiny colored bumps which seemed to protrude everywhere. Almost immediately another door swung aside and something that moved like a man but was obviously made of polished metal came hurrying in, holding something that glowed strangely. Ariadne shrieked and flattened herself against the wall, and the dog cowered, but the giant only smiled and spoke reassuringly in a strange tongue, touching the small girl's shoulder with a surprising gentleness. He turned and spoke to the metal man, and it swiveled to face her, bowing deeply and emitting peculiar clicking sounds. Then, wasting no time, it moved to its master and held out the odd thing it had brought him.

The giant used the tool again to remove the coverings from his hands, and he took the glowing object from the metal man. He held it above his injury, slowly moving it up and down over the entire area. To Ariadne's astonishment the bleeding slowly subsided, and the wound began to close. The giant still seemed tired and weak, but his color was rapidly improving. He sank back in the chair and smiled at the wide-eyed girl.

After a moment he leaned forward again, making encouraging noises to the dog, and it obligingly sidled up to his chair. Taking its bad front leg in his hand, the giant again lifted the glowing thing, moving it round and round over the dog's swollen joint until it began to appear more normal. He stroked the dog, and it leapt up and made several ecstatic circles around the chamber before returning to the girl's side.

Then the giant motioned Ariadne to him, and held the glowing thing out to her. He showed her the little bump that pushed in and made the glow fade away, and he showed her how pushing it again restored the glow. When he seemed to think she understood, he nodded and smiled, pressing the strange thing into her hands and clasping his own great hands over her small ones.

Carefully, then, he rose from the huge chair and tested his leg. Turning to the metal man, he spoke again in that strange dialect, and the doors by which they had entered swung aside. The moving metal strip carried Ariadne and the dog through them, and the metal man went with them as far as the outer doors. While there was still time, Ariadne turned and waved back to the giant and he smiled again, lifting one enormous hand in response. She didn't know who he was, but she was certain she would never see him again.

The dog scampered eagerly ahead, following his own footprints home. Ariadne hurried after him, clutching the gift tightly to her breast; the festival gift which would make her parents well again.

Joe Wehrle, Jr. is a writer and artist. His stories and artwork have appeared in the *Cauliflower Catnip Pearls of Peril, Menomonee Falls Gazette, 1971 Clarion Anthology, Vampirella, Two-Gun Raconteur, Worlds of If, Galaxy, The Digest Enthusiast* and many other publications.

Interviews
Phyllis Galde
Gordon Van Gelder
Matthew Turcotte

Articles
Galaxy Science Fiction
Digest 911
In Defense of Digests
The Big Story
Myron Fass, Foto-rama

Fiction
Lesann Berry
Richard Krauss
Joe Wehrle, Jr.

Interviews
Gary Lovisi
Steve Darnall
Robert Lopresti

Articles
Borderline
Mysterious Traveler
Mister No
Beyond Fantasy Fiction
Australian Crime Digests
Archie Comics Digests

Fiction
D.D. Ploog
Richard Krauss
John Kuharik
Joe Wehrle, Jr.

Interview/Profile
Heather Jacobs
Timothy Green Beckley

Articles
Beyond
Super-Science Fiction
Diabolik
Dashiell Hammett digests
Gunsmoke
Dope Fiends

Fiction
Ron Fortier
Gary Lovisi
Joe Wehrle, Jr.

larquepress.com

Shock Mystery Tales
Overview and Synopses by Peter Enfantino

Naked women and big ugly men. Sadomasochism. Torture chambers. Whips and chains.

I know what you're thinking: just another night at the Kardashians, right? Wrong. These were just a few of the wonderful elements that made up the sleazy package published in 1961 and 1962 as *Shock Mystery Tales* (*SMT*). The publishing history of *SMT* is an interesting one (even if the contents are not): *SMT*, according to Mike Ashley in Michael Cook's *Mystery, Detective, & Espionage Magazines* (Greenwood, 1983), more than likely was spawned from the higher-class *Shock*, published for three issues in 1960 by Winston Publications, out of New York. *Shock* featured some outstanding talent in its short life (albeit mostly reprinted material): Theodore Sturgeon, Henry Kuttner, Ray Bradbury, and Jim Thompson, among others (the latter contributing a new story, thus ensuring a high price tag on the collector's market) but, like most fiction digests of the time, couldn't find a big enough market to keep it alive. So, as with another Winston Publication, *Keyhole Mystery*, the *Shock* title was farmed out to Pontiac Publishing, which held an office at 1 Appleton Street in Holyoke, Massachusetts. If Holyoke rings a bell, that's because it was also home to Headline Publications, which published *Super Science-Fiction* (covered in *TDE3*). More importantly, 1 Appleton Street also spewed out the wild and wonderful whatsis known as *Saturn Science Fiction/Saturn Web Detective/Web Detective/Web Terror Tales*. Whereas the science fiction and detective stories that were featured in the first 18 (of 27) issues were competent and, at times, exemplary, it's the nutty fiction spotlighted in the last eight issues of *Web* that relates to *Shock Mystery Tales*.

Those stories, a combination of babes, bad guys, dungeons and whips, were hardly an innovation.

Web Terror Stories Vol 5 #2 June 1965

They were the same type of stories that dominated the "shudder pulps" of the 1930s and 1940s, and had all but died out.[1] There was, however, a big difference in the twenty years since the shudder pulps. Whereas the women of *Horror Stories*, *Dime Mystery* and *Terror Tales* would get sweaty brows and play peekaboo with a thigh or even (sigh) a milky breast, the broads that populated *Web* and *SMT*, stripped down to their gleaming nakedness in each and every story. The titles in *Web* and *SMT* were very similar to the "shudders" despite the new generation. The 1930s "The Devil's Scalpel," "Coming of the Faceless Killers," "Slave of the Swamp Satan," and "Fresh Fiancés for the Devil's Daughter" gave way to "Soft Hand of Madness," "Orbit of the Pain-Master," "Curse of the Serpent Goddess," and "Handmaidens of the Monster" in the early 1960s.

Through some covert actions and palm-feeding, I was able to unearth a dusty old parchment purporting to be the . . .

Writer's Guidelines for Shock Mystery Tales

1. Introduce the main character
2. Introduce the supporting cast
3. Kidnap the chick
4. Introduce the villain*
5. Introduce the peril
6. Introduce the devices of torture**
7. Strip the chick bare nekkid
8. Introduce pain to her a/nubile, b/sensuous, c/perky, d/firm, or e/delectable flesh
9. Introduce the "out"
10. Tidy expository and fade-out

*The villain should initially be mistaken for a real live ghost, vampire, zombie, ghoul, etc., but is inevitably explained away as just another dirty old man obsessed with bondage and torture, whose parents were burnt at the stake as witches two hundred years before.

**Devices of torture should include, but not be limited to, whip, cat o' nine tails, iron maiden, pendulum, DVD box sets of *Touched By An Angel* episodes, etc.

A lot of the writers for *SMT* also

---

1 If you're interested in the history of the "shudder pulps," there are a few great references if you're inclined to search them out on eBay. The fanzines, *Echoes* and *Xenophile*, carried pieces on the "shudders" now and then, but these zines are getting scarcer and scarcer. The most complete history to date, between two covers that is, would have to be *The Shudder Pulps* by Robert Kenneth Jones (FAX, 1975), a fondly nostalgic rambling that I couldn't put down. There may be better written and more informative volumes in the future, but Jones' book does the trick for now.

appeared in the other Holyoke zines. Bill Ryder wrote over two dozen stories for *SMT*, *Web*, *Off-Beat*, and *Two-Fisted* (the latter published by Reese Publishing, an offshoot of Pontiac—let me know when this gets confusing), but his work for *SMT* was nothing stellar; Alan Lance also saw stories featured in *Guilty*, published by Feature Publications (an offshoot of, all together now, Pontiac/Reese/Headline/Candar/ etc.), a slightly more upscale crime digest than those catering to the S&M crowd; and the king of them all, Art Crockett, who saw print with nearly 50 stories in the crime digests, with some of his work in the finer-smelling pages of *Manhunt* and *Mike Shayne*. Most, if not all, of the 30 stories that ran in the 512 pages of *Shock Mystery Tales* read like rejects for the "classier" Holyoke pubs:

"George Sebold's eyes laughed."

"Her firm young breasts had risen and fallen with her agitated breathing . . . hurriedly, she had stripped and jumped under the shower. The cool water cascaded over her lush nudeness, calming her jangled nerves."

"The tunnel was full of an overpowering chemical essence. It stung like Benzine Hexachloride Gammaxane and some of the other new plant stimulants."

"Vulpe's whip snapped again. This time Phyllis' silk skirt cascaded down around her bound ankles. She stood before the beast incarnate, her voluptuous young figure hidden only in the sheerest nylon panties and bra. The covering hid nothing from the fiend, but served to inflame his diabolically warped desires. The vicious whip whirled around her breasts and then her waist. Vulpe

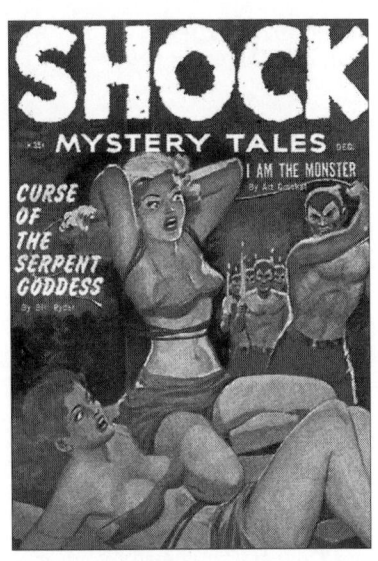

Shock Mystery Tales Vol 2 #1 December 1961

was systematically stripping the bound girl with the hellish lash."

"As we danced, I could feel her breasts thrust tight and proud against my chest, and through the sleazy [sic] material of her form-fitting sheath my hands told me that she wore no undergarments."

SMT had some wonderful advertisers as well. You could order the "Suspens-O-Truss" from the Kinlen Company out of Kansas City. Kinlen guaranteed the Truss would provide "double relief and comfort for the rupture sufferer." You could order the "Birth Spacing System," approved and sanctioned by churches, a "compact slide-rule that can tell a woman when you may become pregnant—and when you are not fertile!" I won't sleep until I lay my hands on a copy of *Flagellation and the Flagellants*, a "history of the rod in all countries," newly revised by William Cooper.

Obviously, *Shock Mystery Tales* is not for all tastes.

Shock Mystery Tales
Vol. 2 #1 December 1961

Brides for the Devil's Cauldron
by Don Unatin (7800 words)

Three young beauties accidentally run over a mountain girl and the girl's father vows the three will burn in hell. Shortly thereafter, the girls disappear. When next we meet up with them, they're hanging naked over a burning pit. Lots of naked blistering flesh and whip burns.

I Am the Monster
by Art Crockett (9000 words)

Barry dreams he becomes a beastly character named Avram at night and ravages his fiancé while she sleeps. This escalates to murder and Barry finds it very hard to enjoy his sleep. This story and the preceding one perfectly illustrate the problem *SMT*'s editor (whoever the hell he might have been) had in discerning a novelette (as "Brides" was labelled) from a short story (the designation for "Monster") in spite of the fact that "Brides" is over 1000 words longer than "Monster."

Curse of the Serpent Goddess
by Bill Ryder (8100 words)

A newspaper reporter falls under the spell of a nightclub performer, Conchita, the titular serpent goddess. Seems Conchita wants Greg to join her merry band of zombie slaves, but true love wills out and Greg fights off Conchita's hypnotic powers before burying a dagger into the naked quivering flesh of his fiancé. Throughout the story we're led to believe that Conchita may just be of serpent background, but the finale's laughable explanation (one that would have made Velma of *Scooby-Doo* proud) points to Conchita as just another love-lust hussy. Everything about this story cries out "Low-budget Universal horror of the 1950s," such as :

"I looked up again. I staggered backwards in my chair. The clock's face had been replaced by the vision of Conchita. Her blood red lips curled back in a mirthless smirk of victory."

Vengeance of the Undead
by Anthony Stuart (4700 words)

Salim's got a torture chamber (who doesn't?) and he intends to put it to good use when he captures the last remaining member of the family that put to death his great-great-grandparents. The naked blistering flesh adds a nice unique approach.

Hell's Photographer
by Jim Burnett (5600 words)

Curt Simpson is the most revered photographer in the United States. He's also a bondage freak who loves to torture his favorite subjects until they're naked, bleeding and dead. Enter Merilee, a beautiful model with no brains and big plans. One of the few *SMT* stories that doesn't include blistering nakedness (I kinda missed it actually).

The Damned of Terror Island
by Jim Arthur (7500 words)

Ace newspaper photog Chet Morgan is convinced that eccentric millionaire Jason Trundle is up to something fishy on his private island. Turns out Trundle is kidnapping hookers and burning them alive as sacrifices to his hooded followers.

Her Killer's Waiting
by Seymour Shubin (1400 words)

When a woman shows up at his precinct voicing concern that her husband plans to kill her, Detective Stone has no choice but to agree to talk to the man, little knowing the woman has actually set a trap to rid herself of her abusive husband.

Shock Mystery Tales Vol. 2 #2 March 1962

Soft Hands of Madness
by Bill Ryder (8000 words)

Margaret Dillard, the new nurse at Dr. Gruber's mental institution, begins to suspect something's up when the patients keep screaming gibberish about hands and the basement. Gruber's assistant Greta Himmelsdorf is a Nazi war criminal conducting experiments on Gruber's patients. A rare tale told in first-person from a female perspective. Liberal doses of the typical S&M, torture chambers and mad scientists, with a twist of subtle lesbianism thrown in for good measure.

Satan's Mistress
by Craighton Lamont (7400 words)

Theo and Margie O'Malley manage to make a wrong turn somewhere in Ireland and end up in the small town of Bynagh. Ignoring speed limit signs, Theo is pulled over by the local constable and the couple is hauled off to jail... or what they think is a jail. The police actually take Theo and Margie to a castle, where hooded Nazis prepare a *SMT* version of *The Manchurian Candidate*. A rare good story, despite the necessary breast implants and lacy panties. The

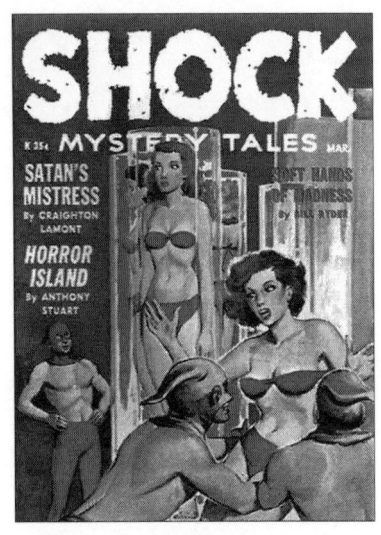

Shock Mystery Tales Vol 2 #2 March 1962

story does have its sense of humor:

"His eyes were hooded and cruel and his whole expression was theatrically sardonic as though he'd just been advised by prepaid cable that the late Adolf Hitler had been his uncle."

The Devil's Caress
by William H. Duhart (3400 words)

Mafia man George Sebold is bound and determined to get Gloria Hanson, M.D. in the sack. Gloria sidesteps him, but when Sebold attempts rape, the woman cracks.

Lust of the Jungle Goddess
by Bob Shields (8200 words)

Rider Morrison and his Psychical Research team are combing the jungles of North America in search of voodoo. What they find is voodoo queen Ormulu and her vicious Hawk Men. What they're up to, I can't tell you, other than to reiterate that *SMT* has a lot of naked glistening flesh amidst its crumbling pages.

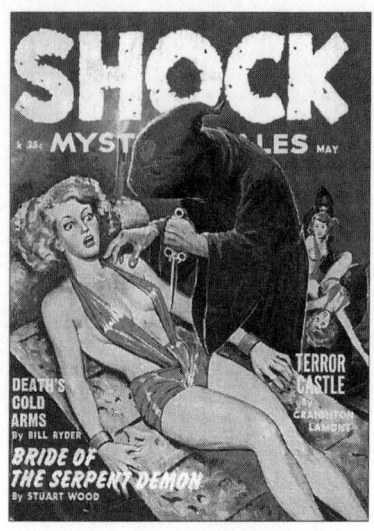

Shock Mystery Tales Vol 2 #3 May 1962

Brides of Pain
by Jim Burnett (8400 words)
Gary and Ruth spend their honeymoon in hell with the sadistic Señor and Señora Mureda, cabin owners who add a little something to a couple's weekend: torture. Incredibly gory tale which exists only to titillate those who live for stuff like Jeffrey Dahmer trading cards.

Black Chapel
by Larry Dickson (800 words)
Docudrama about witch sightings in Salem in the 17th Century.

Horror Island
by Anthony Stuart (8700 words)
A botanist and his crew happen to crack their boat up on the reef of an island belonging to the famous Japanese war criminal, Dr. Kimpei Sueyoshi (proof that *SMT* was indeed politically correct), who's concocted a killer fungus to destroy the world (think Fool Manchu).

"Horror Island" is a lot of fun, with heaping ingredients of what makes shudder pulps popular even today: the crazed scientist (who "resembles a human praying mantis") with steel pincers in lieu of hands, a bloodsucking squid, and giant centipedes. Stuart's descriptions of the florid horrors the men discover on the island tend to be a bit embellished:

"Huge, man-thick trunks soared fifty feet in the air, trunks warted and noduled with masses of parasitical fungi. Great fluted fangs of smooth-surfaced umber spread on either side of us. Vast fungoid eruptions and excrescences loomed beside us like monstrous boils on the leperous-colored earth. Things spread out in venomous splotched yellow greens like enormous fungivorous octopi, waiting with thousands of warted suckers to trap the unwary."

Shock Mystery Tales Vol. 2 #3 May 1962

Terror Castle!
by Craighton Lamont (7300 words)
Craig Saxon marries into millions when he courts ex-prostitute Bunny Moscowitz Murray. While vacationing abroad, the couple is kidnapped and tortured by Bunny's angry uncle, torqued about being left out of the will.

Curse of the Undead!
by James Barnett (9400 words)
Way back in 1925, the otherwise gentle townfolk of Middlebury lynched the murdering rapist known only as "Young Gower." Beside his twisting, mutilated corpse, his old crony witch mother

swears vengeance on the virgin daughters of her son's executioners. Nearly 40 years later, the town's new school teacher sees the old lady's curse unfolding before her supple, glistening eyes.

Black Chapel!
by Larry Dickson (1600 words)
In the second installment of this pseudo-history of sadism through the ages, we're enlightened to the benefits of burying one's victims alive, as well as the fine arts of boiling, pressing and crucifixion.

Death's Cold Arms!
by Bill Ryder (7300 words)
It's apparent that Ilene Masters is the latest victim of the Masters curse, which has killed off all of the Masters, save one, Lynn, who has all but resigned herself to death. Of course, we readers know by page three (at least those of us who have read any of the SMT stories) that two facts are apparent: Lynn will feel the chill air on her naked flesh and that it's really Uncle Malcolm who's killing off the Masters so that he may (all together now) claim the Masters' inheritance.

Bride of the Serpent Demon!
by Stuart Wood (7300 words)
The nameless narrator has dame problems. First he picks up Angelina, a "sultry, unusually developed teen-aged girl" with a fondness for snakes. When he gets over her (the next day), he falls madly in love with Nanette, who (coincidentally?) turns out to be Angelina's roommate. When the stud confronts Angelina with the news that he and Nanette will soon be married, the vixen drops a bombshell right on his manhood:
"Do you mean to say she hasn't told you," she sneered into my face.
"Told me what?"
"Nanette's a lesbian. We—"
"O, my god!"
But it doesn't matter to this Romeo because "when she was in my arms, she behaved normally." Turns out that Angelina is not only an Ellen DeGeneres admirer, but a devil snake worshipper to boot and intends to make Nanette her latest sacrifice. Pretty risqué mix of lesbianism, three-way sex, and snake charming. Contrary to popular belief, this is not a sequel to "Curse of the Serpent Goddess."

Lovely Maiden From Hell!
by Anthony Stuart (7000 words)
What is the secret of Karamaneh Siva, the famous actress known for her steamy role in the cult classic *Satan's Mistress*? She seems to be older than her years, but our hero soon digs up dirt on our lovely maiden—Siva drains and drinks the blood of kidnapped girls to retain her beauty and youth.

Lust of the Vampire Queen!
by Alan Lance (4100 words)
Newlyweds Dan and Darla stop off at the Museum of Hollywood Horrors, owned and operated by the famous Monica Le Vine, star of 27 vampire movies. Evidently the vampire stuff finally got to Monica, because now she just sits in her museum and waits for young beauties to come along so she can slaughter them and drink their blood, ensuring the continuation of her good looks.

Shock Mystery Tales
Vol. 2 #4 July 1962

Soft Brides for the Damned!
by James Barnett (8900 words)

Covering society for *The Clarion*, ace newspaper person Judy Townshend witnesses first hand the cruelty inflicted upon Dr. Snipe (of the Wilmer Home for Crippled Men) by the women of the Midview Country Club. The last laughs belong to Dr. Snipe, however, when he commands his merry men to kidnap and torture all the women who mocked him. This includes our ace reporter, who deep down had felt sympathy for the doc, but will get naked and tortured regardless. The *SMT* Theatre version of Tod Browning's *Freaks*, "Soft Brides" is filled with wonderfully pulpish sentences:

"This couldn't happen. This was the 20th Century. A group of freaks couldn't suddenly descend on an apartment development, hogtie a woman, and carry her off into the night."

"I knew this phase of my abduction was like nothing which was to come."

"Her magnificent breasts strained upwards towards the ceiling."

Black Chapel!
by Richard Shaw (2400 words)

The third and final installment takes a look at poltergeists. No raw naked flesh in sight.

Vengeance of the Devil's Mistress!
by Art Crockett (6400 words)

Rod Porter, a "television scenic developer," and his main squeeze, are scouting backgrounds for an upcoming TV show on witchcraft when they stumble onto a mysterious old woman on a dark country road.

Handmaidens of the Monster!
by Alan Lance (4500 words)

Evil Professor Demal has been creating frog-girls and rat-men for Hollywood monster movies. A special effects man is on to him though, and soon brings the walls crashing down on the mad scientist's film career. So where are the handmaidens?

Evil Stalks the Night!
by F. X. Fallon (3000 words)

Psychopath Billy wanders from town to town, murdering young girls and dumping their bodies in the forest. His travels lead him to the farm house of kindly Ma and Pa Pembley, a wonderful old couple, still grieving the loss of their son, also named Billy. Before Billy can realize what's going on, he's locked in the cellar, doomed to be the Pembleys' little boy forever. Not bad, but definitely out of place in *SMT* since there are no threatened couples or torture devices. I suspect that this was a story originally slated for *SMT*'s sister publication, *Web Detective Stories* until the "Detective" was dropped in favor of its replacement, "Terror."

Night of the Walking Dead!
by Jim Arthur (4600 words)

Cataleptic George Peterson is nearly buried alive by his wife and her lover. When George's servant grows suspicious and digs George up in the proverbial nick of time, George (naturally) emerges with a large chip on his shoulder (understandably). He buries the two lovers alive but (ironically) is struck with a

Shock Mystery Tales

bout of catalepsy just as he's unloading the last shovelful of dirt. Lying seemingly dead, George is eaten (gruesomely) by vultures. Like the preceding story, a change of pace for *SMT*, "Night" most resembles an oft-told EC horror comics story.

In the Name of Terror
by Larry Dickson (2200 words)
The Crypt Speaks!
by Harvey Berg (1300 words)

Two companion pieces to "The Black Chapel," "In the Name of Terror" tells the story of voodoo in Haiti, while "The Crypt Speaks" of ghostly visits.

Satan's Ballet!
by Bill Ryder (9800 words)

The maestro himself, Antoine Duval, has conceived of the ultimate dance show, The Mephisto Ballet, and beautiful Mercedes St. Clair is trapped amidst the orgy when all hell breaks loose. Now this is more like the *SMT* we've come to expect—"burning brimstone on naked flesh" and "the sensuous undulation of unfettered hips."

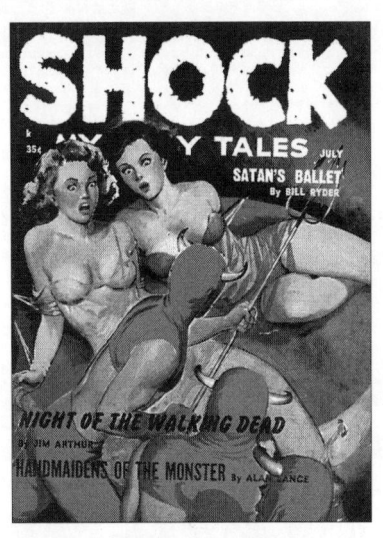

Shock Mystery Tales Vol 2 #4 July 1962

Peter Enfantino is an obsessive collector of Mystery, Crime and Horror digests including *Alfred Hitchcock*, *Manhunt*, *Mike Shayne*, as well as the entire stable of Warren Magazines. He has written for all the major channels on the topics, including *Paperback Parade*, *Mystery Scene*, *Mystery File*, *Comic Effect*, and Peter Normanton's *From the Tomb*. For thirteen years he co-edited *The Scream Factory* and *Bare Bones* magazines, and currently blogs at bare·bones e-zine. He divides his time between Mesa, AZ and London, England. ∠ ∠

Cartoon by Bob Vojtko, caption by R. Krauss

"Housebound misogynist seeks voluptuous virgin runaway for piercing, marking and cleansing. One night only."

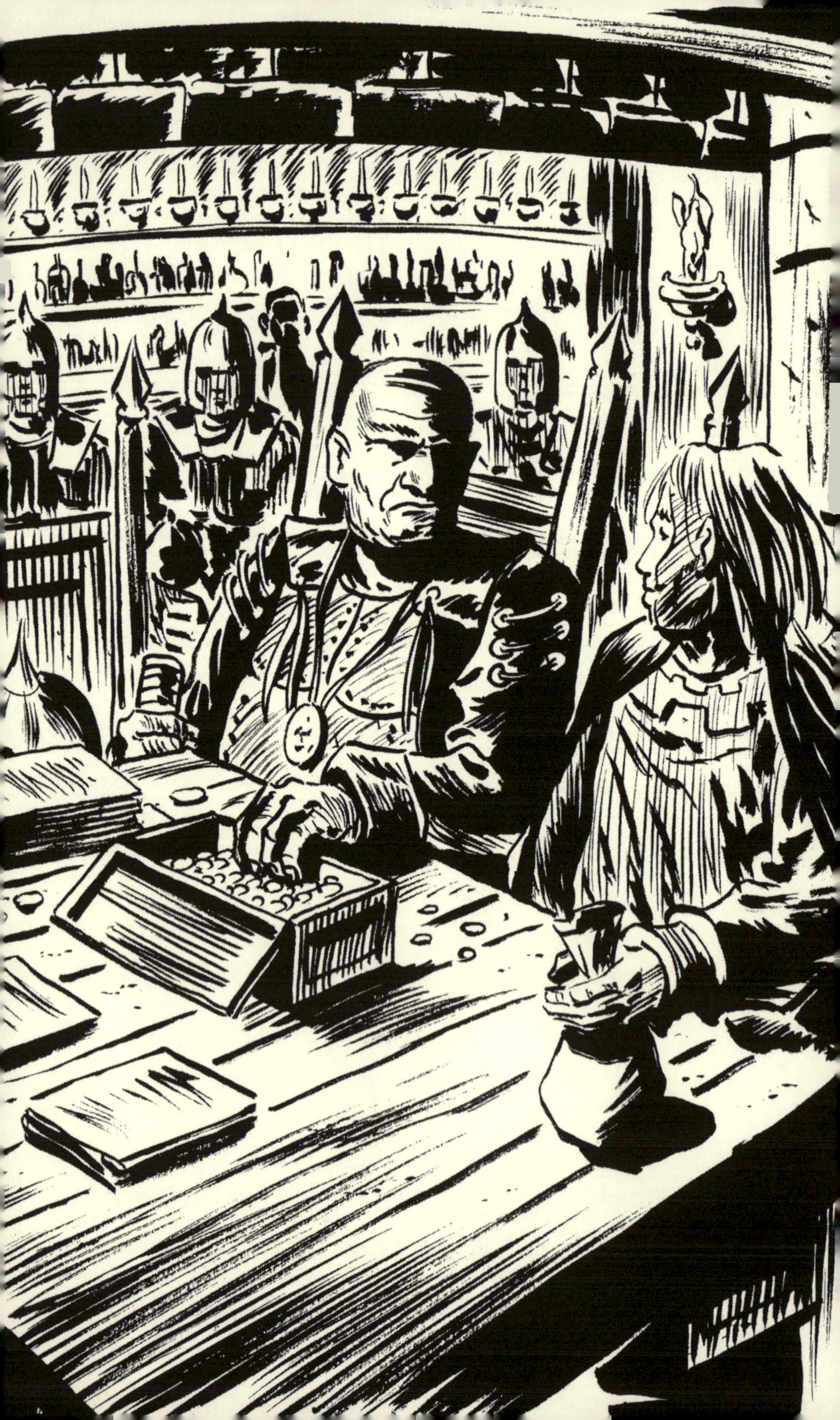

Wounded Wizard
Fantasy fiction by John M. Kuharik
Illustrations by Michael Neno

Captain Lars of the NightWatch sat at a table in the Round Keg Tavern. Candles lit the walls of the room. A fireplace crackled across from the bar. A cashbox rested near his left hand, a short sword near his right. A sheaf of papers lay in front of him. He wore black leather armor and the King's medallion on a chain around his neck. A helmet sat on the chair to his right. A shaven head and dark eyebrows gave him a fierce countenance. Four of his men stood at the bar, clubs prominent on their belts.

When the Gnolls came over the lower walls and spilled into the streets of Buckthorn Burrough, its residents were ready for them.

Men alongside women, these descendants of border ranchers joined their local militiamen to fight with swords and garden tools against the charging beasts. But commanders of the regular army within the castle walls, doubting their ability, unleashed a mortar attack upon friend and foe alike. The population and buildings were devastated. When the fires cooled, the Gnolls were defeated, but a once thriving community was now a ragged assortment of wounded veterans, resentful homeless, and gangs of hungry orphans.

Grigg, a competent swordsman, and Ladwick, an able wizard, had been fighting with the Buckthorn militia when the mortar rounds from the castle landed around them. Grigg caught shrapnel in his left arm and leg, but kept fighting. Ladwick, in a group closer to the explosion, was blasted unconscious and knocked into a coma for days.

"You still look like the blonde god you always were," said Grigg, at Ladwick's bedside when he finally awoke. Indeed, the wizard had no outward injuries. But he complained of headaches, and seemed overwhelmed with an unfamiliar sadness and lethargy.

As weeks passed, Grigg decided to make an effort to help his friend "soldier on through," as he liked to say. He earned a living now doing what he liked best—looting the old battlefields for lost and broken armor which he repaired and resold—and doing what he didn't like as well, odd jobs for war widows running farms on the plains west of the Burrough. To get Ladwick moving, he told him he had more work than he could handle. "I've got jobs with widows lined up for a month."

At first reluctant, Ladwick went along on a few jobs and seemed to be getting his physical strength back at least.

On a particular day, Grigg had led them out of the city along a wagon road that cut through low grass and sage brush to the widow Barlow's farm. She had sent word she needed someone to find her lost sheep.

"I know what you're doing," said Ladwick.

"What?"

"You're dragging me along because you think it's good for me." He turned in the saddle to face Grigg. "There isn't any job we've done out here that you couldn't do as fast by yourself. You don't need me, and I sure don't need your charity or your pity."

Grigg stroked his clean shaven chin, undaunted in his desire to help his friend. "Well, I don't know about charity or pity, but I do know a lazy son-of-a-bitch feeling sorry for himself when I see him."

"You have no idea what you're talking about," said Ladwick.

They tied their horses to a tree in a grove, and climbed a short hill to get a view of the surrounding area. Upon reaching the top, it was difficult to say who was more surprised, Grigg and Ladwick, or the band of bloody-faced Gnolls who were sitting in a pile of bloody wool, eating the sheep in question.

Gnolls resemble wolves by virtue of fangs, claws, and fur, but they differ by walking upright, wearing armor, and using hand weapons. This band was obviously a remnant of the Gnoll army that had been defeated in the Burrough last summer.

The Gnolls looked up, grabbed their swords and axes, and rushed to encircle the men.

"I suppose you think I arranged this Gnoll attack for your benefit?"

"I wouldn't put it past you."

Grigg stripped off his cloak, and with his right hand drew a large saber from a sheath on his back. He drew a short sword from his waist with his other, and took a fighting stance there on the high ground, looking taller than his six feet. As the beasts closed on him, he became a virtual whirlwind of massive muscles, slicing off limbs, ripping open stomachs, and detaching heads. Torn arteries spurted blood in all directions.

Ladwick stood behind him in his gray robe, arms extended, channeling every ounce of his wizardly power to provide a magical shield that kept the Gnolls from attacking from behind. Every so often the shield would waver and he would yell "on the left," or "on the right," to let Grigg know a beast had slipped around one side. Soon, both men were sweating despite the chill of the day. Ten beasts lay dead in front of Grigg, one was crawling away, its hind quarters useless. Two others continued their maniacal assault. One had sunken its teeth into the leather armor protecting Grigg's left forearm. The teeth had not penetrated skin, but the beast's weight dragged the arm down making it useless. Grigg sliced the standing Gnoll across the throat. It grabbed its neck with both hands and started choking on gushing blood. Keeping an eye on it, Grigg began striking the head of the beast attached to his arm with the hilt of the saber. Three strikes rendered the thing senseless, but it took a violent shaking on his part to make it let go. As it flopped to the ground, Grigg ran it through the heart with the short sword, and with a curse, did the same to the choking one yet to fall.

"Clear back here," said Ladwick.

"The same," said Grigg, eyes reviewing the carnage to be sure. Both men were splattered with Gnoll blood. Grigg drove the saber into the ground in front of him and turned to clasp Ladwick's hand in victory. "We still got it."

"You still got it," said Ladwick, bending forward, hands on his knees, breathing hard, "but I've lost it." More deep breaths. "Hell, I used to cast fireballs. Look at me now. It takes all I got just to cast a small shield. You don't believe me, but my brain is gone."

"Come on, stop feeling sorry for yourself. Your brain is fine." Grigg grabbed his friend under one arm, standing him up. They gathered the Gnoll weapons in silence and secured them to the horses.

"Let's tell the widow about her sheep, and head for home. A mug or two of ale, and you'll feel like your old self."

"That's the problem, Grigg. And, it proves you don't understand that I can't be my old self. That self is gone—gone in the blast. Just saying have a mug of ale and feel like your old self, won't make it so."

They mounted their horses.

"You know what? Don't come around anymore. Thanks for being friends with who I used to be, but I'm sorry, he's gone. I'm not him. I don't know who I am." Turning, he spurred his horse for home.

Grigg settled with the widow Barlow, then followed his friend at a distance into Buckthorn. He reached his house at dusk and felt annoyed to see a man standing near his door, obviously waiting for him.

"Who are you?" he asked as he dismounted. The man stepped from the shadows, and Grigg saw he wore a NightWatch badge and had a club hooked to his belt.

"Captain Lars wants to see you."

"I'm busy this week."

"He wants to see you now."

"What about?"

"No idea." The man took a friendlier tone. "You know how he is. Why make life difficult for yourself? He's at his usual place."

Captain Lars of the NightWatch sat at a table in the Round Keg Tavern. Candles lit the walls of the room. A fireplace crackled across from the bar. A cashbox rested near his left hand, a short sword near his right. A sheaf of papers lay in front of him. He wore black leather armor and the King's medallion on a chain around his neck. A helmet sat on the chair to his right. A shaven head and dark eyebrows gave him a fierce countenance. Four of his men stood at the bar, clubs prominent on their belts.

The tavern served as Lars' headquarters, the place he conducted the King's business. He received a royal stipend with which he paid himself and the men he recruited into the NightWatch. He granted business licenses, travel visas, and work permits—all said to be required by the king, all requiring a fee paid to Lars.

He was physically imposing even when seated. His battlefield prowess was legendary. Some thought his rage against the Gnolls was admirable, even patriotic, but Grigg, having served under the man in the militia, suspected he was simply homicidal. He seemed too eager to deal out capital punishment to his own men for offenses other commanders would consider minor.

When Grigg arrived at the Round Keg, several people stood in line in front of Lars' table, with heads bowed, and with coins in their sweaty palms. They hoped to get permits for jobs in the castle. Grigg sprawled into the chair on Lars' left.

"So, I'm here."

Lars continued writing without looking up. "You've become an insolent son-of-a-bitch," he said quietly. "You think you can disrespect me in front of everyone, any time you want? Your day is coming, Griggsy."

A man gave over a coin which Lars threw so hard into the cashbox that it bounced out onto the floor. A man at the bar scurried to pick it up.

"You aren't my commanding officer anymore," Grigg said, also quietly.

"If you had acted like this back then, I'd have had you hung."

"Then was then, now is now. What do you want, Lars?"

"I got a job for you. If I had anyone—anyone—else I thought could do this, I'd give it to them in a minute." He dropped a small bag of coins on the table. "Ten gold now, ten more upon completion." He leaned into Grigg's ear. "It's a rescue. Damsel in distress. Right down your alley."

Grigg grunted.

Lars leaned back in his chair. "An heiress named Melissa went missing from the castle. Day before her wedding, blah, blah, blah. The family gets a ransom note. They follow directions and drop the money at the cemetery. The money disappears, but the girl is not returned. Now her old man is twice as pissed."

"Ok, I'm interested. Where do I start?"

"Informants tell me that a sin-eater named Crowdine knows something. But no one can find her when she isn't actually eating sins. She hides near the cemetery."

Grigg scowled. "A sin-eater?

That's your best lead, seriously? The sin-eater is always the first one the nobles hang for anything they can't blame on anyone else."

Lars leaned forward and stuck a finger in Grigg's face. "What do you care? Twenty gold is a fortune. Find this Crowdine. Find out what she knows. If she won't tell you anything, bring her here. I've got ways to make her talk."

"Why not send your own men?"

Lars tapped a finger on the desk, hesitating a moment. "I did. Two different guys." He looked at his men standing at the bar. "They never came back. I need someone resourceful, like you."

An image of the cemetery with its ornate tombstones flashed through Grigg's mind. Only nobles from the castle were buried there. Commoners from Buckthorn were buried in backyards and empty lots. In the event of mass casualties, as during the recent war—the dead went into a common grave near the river.

Also, only rich people used sin-eaters. It was a practice where food was placed in special dishes directly on the corpse just before the burial. A sin-eater was then invited to pull up a chair and eat the food, and by so doing, absorb all the sins from the deceased, allowing him or her to enter the afterlife with a pure soul. Grigg supposed rich people thought they could buy a ticket to anywhere.

Often a small bag of coins was left near the food as an unspoken way of insuring the sin-eater's silence about the sins discovered. The risk for the sin-eater came from still living fellow sinners of the deceased—partners-in-crime and the like—who might not feel that a small bag of coins was enough to insure silence, and would attempt to achieve a more permanent solution. The disappearance of a particular sin-eater was never, ever, noticed. Another always rose from the ranks of the destitute before the next funeral rolled around.

The day after meeting Lars, Grigg walked to Ladwick's house and knocked on the door. "You in there? I got us a job at the cemetery."

Ladwick wouldn't open his door. "Go away," he said.

"Come on, we gotta talk to a sin-eater."

"I said go away, Grigg. I told you I'm not going out on your jobs anymore."

"Come on. It's a sin-eater, for crying out loud."

"Good bye, Grigg."

The cemetery lay against the castle wall, nine blocks up and four over from Grigg's house. River fog overspread the area keeping it cool. He passed very few people, which reminded him of the heavy casualties Buckthorn had suffered in the war. And that reminded him of Ladwick. Preoccupied with these thoughts he failed to notice shadowy figures moving in the broken windows and doors of the buildings lining the street. A rock hitting the wall near his head got his attention. Damn orphans. He quickened his pace, until a hail of rocks made him break into a full run. He arrived at the cemetery sweaty, and in a foul mood.

He walked among the tombstones until he came upon the bent-backed caretaker shoveling dirt into a grave. He waited until the man finished.

"How do I find the

sin-eater?" he asked.

"Who are you?" asked the man, adjusting his gloves.

Grigg pulled out a silver coin. "Do you know where I can find Crowdine the sin-eater or not?"

"No one knows where she lives." He took the coin. "No one wants to know. I post the funeral times on the front gate, and she shows up."

"When's the next funeral?"

"Got two funerals today. One in an hour, and another after lunch."

Grigg left the cemetery and found a tavern a block away. He drank coffee while he watched and waited for the funeral to begin. Soon enough, well dressed people started arriving in carriages from the castle. Grigg noticed he could easily pass as a driver or bodyguard among this group, so he stepped into the street and followed a noble couple walking from their parked carriage.

Reaching the grave site, he saw the sin-eater was half finished with her meal. She perched on a bench wearing a burlap cloak with the hood up. He saw her dirty face and straggly brown hair when she turned sideways for a moment. She leaned forward over the dishes on the corpse, and ate slowly with her fingers, as though the sins were difficult to chew and swallow. The mourners huddled in groups, and pretended not to look at her. Finishing, she wiped her mouth on her sleeve, picked up a handful of bread and a small bag of coins and headed to the street. The crowd gave her plenty of room. Women covered their noses with handkerchiefs.

He followed her discreetly two blocks into a narrow passageway between deserted stores. She never looked back as she wove her way among several homeless figures lying huddled in rags. She paused at one, where she stooped and put pieces of bread into its coat pocket. Then moved on until she disappeared behind a nondescript door.

Grigg decided to take a straightforward approach with her. Without drawing a weapon, he knocked quietly. He heard a chair scrape, then nothing. He knocked again. More silence. He tried the handle and the door eased open inwardly by itself. The sun chose that moment to emerge from the fog, and cast a shaft of sunlight into the room. He stepped in and noticed, too late, that a figure to his right was holding a crossbow. A woman's voice said, "Close the door."

"Easy with that thing," he said.

"I said close the door."

Grigg, noticing the bow was cocked with a bolt aimed at his guts, closed the door and stood motionless.

"I didn't come here to hurt you."

"Oh, unlike the other two?"

"I had nothing to do with them. I knocked politely on your door, and have no sword in my hand." His eyes locked on the bolt in the crossbow noticing it had a military style head with jagged barbs. He guessed it would easily penetrate his leather at this range.

"So, why are you here?"

He decided to continue with the truth. "The NightWatch hired me to find someone named Crowdine and talk to her about a missing heiress . . . Melissa by name."

The woman said nothing.

"Most of those have a hair trigger," said Grigg, nodding to her weapon.

More silence as she sized him up.

"You are Crowdine aren't you?"

Suddenly, several things happened at once. The door burst open with a bang and the shaft of sunlight re-entered the room. The woman jumped, and the crossbow went off. Grigg blinked in surprise at who had opened the door and heard the jagged-barbed bolt whiz past his left ear and stick into the wall behind him.

"Ladwick?"

The woman quickly set the nose of her weapon on the floor, and stepped on the bow to re-cock it.

"I'm only here because you're in a world of shit," said Ladwick. "Don't pretend you know you were followed."

Grigg stepped toward the woman and snatched the crossbow. "I told you it had a hair trigger." Then to his friend, "I was followed?"

"I looked out the window after you left my house this morning, and saw two guys on your tail. I decided to follow your followers, and here I am." He paused and looked at the woman, who struggled against Grigg trying to get her hands on the crossbow. "So is this the heiress?"

Grigg and the woman stopped struggling. "No, this is Crowdine the sin-eater."

"Heiress? Sin-eater? Same thing, right honey?" asked Ladwick.

Crowdine/Melissa said, "I'm not your honey." But then seemed to sag as she put her hands over her face.

Ladwick went on. "I got the story from one of the men following you." He jerked a thumb over his shoulder. "Don't worry. He's laying in the alley, and will be for a while."

Grigg smiled to Crowdine/Melissa, "He's a wizard. He has a special way with people."

"If I may continue, Lars thinks Melissa here staged her own kidnapping." He turned to her, "He guessed who you really are when one of his spies saw a kid from the castle pulling on your shawl and calling you Melissa at a funeral. At first, he wanted you for the ransom money you stole. But when your father offered a huge new reward, he hatched a new plan. And that's where you come in, Grigg. Lars is setting you up to take the blame for the kidnapping. They are going to catch you with Crowdine, have a quick trial, and string you up." Ladwick pretended to dust off his hands. "Lars gets to be the law-and-order hero, gets the reward money and, maybe best of all for him . . . gets rid if you."

"I never meant to get anyone else in trouble," said Melissa. "I'll tell them I ran away, which I did."

Grigg took it all in quickly. "No, you're doomed. He counted off on his fingers. One, a sin-eater. Two, a ransom stealer. Three, a disobedient daughter. They'd kill you for any one of those. All three? Forget it. Lars is giving them a story they can believe—and will want to believe."

The men looked at Melissa expecting her to add to the story.

"All right," she said. "I didn't know until recently that my father isn't my father. What kid thinks something like that? Life was great. Turns out though, I'm nothing more than a fancy slave. A slave he now wants to marry off to a smelly old man who owns a bunch of smelly old boats."

The men looked quizical.

"He owns the freight docks on the river and most of the barges. My father will get half his business after the wedding."

"So, if you aren't your father's daughter, who are you?"

"He brought me home from a war in the mountains out west." She blushed, "And it seems everyone knew this while I was growing up, except me. I've been a real fool."

Grigg said, "Must have been the The High Steppes Wars."

"Sounds about right," said Ladwick.

"What?" she asked.

"You might be from the High Steppes. The castle was at war with them when we were young."

Ladwick had grown impatient. "I'm sure Lars and his men are closing in on us. How are we going to get her out of this, Grigg?"

"I have one more question. What happened to the real Crowdine?"

"Oh," Melissa looked pained. "When I first came here, she let me stay with her. But when I brought in the ransom money, it scared her. She took her own coins and left the city that night."

"And where's the ransom now?"

"I have it."

Grigg nodded, then opened the door to the alley and looked out. "You know that homeless guy you gave bread to?"

"Yeah, Jayce, he's a friend."

"Let's get him in here, and change his clothes."

Mourners began to arrive for the second funeral of the day. A meal had been spread out over the corpse. Right on schedule, the sin-eater, wearing a hooded, burlap shawl, arrived and and made for the body. The nobles turned their faces away as usual.

Having finally finished, the sin-eater rose and made for the street. The mourners made room. At the cemetery gates, Grigg emerged from behind a stone pillar, and grabbed the sin-eater by the arm. He whispered, "Steady now, Jayce. Just play along like we said, and the gold I promised is yours." But in a louder voice, easily heard by Lars' men he pretended not to know were hidden in nearby doorways he said, "Come along with me, Crowdine. I need to talk to you."

Lars' men rushed out on cue. Some seized Grigg and others, noticeably reluctant, seized the sin-eater they thought was Crowdine. Grigg put up a faux struggle creating enough noise to attract attention from the nobles in the cemetery. Lars walked up then and pulled off the sin-eater's hood, expecting to reveal Melissa posing as Crowdine.

But there stood the straggly-haired Jayce, still belching and now blinking in the sunlight. The men holding him let go.

"What is this?" asked Lars. "Who are you?"

"I'm the sin-eater."

Lars looked at Grigg, who said, "I'm as surprised as you are, Captain. I thought this was the Crowdine character."

By now several men from the funeral had come near to see what the comotion was.

Lars said under his breath "This is your doing."

Grigg spread his hands, "I don't know what you mean."

Lars to his men, "Spread out and find her."

Grigg said, "I'm as disappointed as you, Captain. You paid me tengold to find Crowdine, and its not her. Here's your money back."

"You are a sly one, Grigg." Lars grabbed the bag of coins. "This isn't over."

"May I go sir?" asked

Jayce, head bowed.

Lars spit on the ground. "You're going to get yours too, you piece of shit." Jayce hurried away.

Meanwhile, blocks away from the action at the cemetery gate, Ladwick and Melissa hurried through a weeded lot hoping to make it back to his house unseen. She carried a pack with her clothes and the ransom gold. He had cast a spell to make her load weightless, even though it caused him a headache to keep it up.

"You're the first wizard I've seen without a magic staff," she observed.

"It got blown up in the war. New ones are hard to come by."

The NightWatch seemed everywhere. Before long, a small group sighted them.

"Can't you do something about them?"

"I have a brain injury. I might make one forget he'd seen us, but I can't handle a bunch. We gotta run."

They crossed the street and moved onto a path weaving through ruins of burnt houses. Ladwick seemed to know the way by heart. When he kept glancing back at her, she said, "Just run, I'll keep up."

One deserted street after another, they eventually ducked into a blackened factory and rested until Ladwick caught sight of riders flanking them off to the right. His headache was making him dizzy.

"Are we going somewhere, or just running?" she asked.

"Somewhere," he managed to say. They ran, angling left through more ruins, until they reached a cul-de-sac. Holding still, they listened for their followers. "It's important they don't see what we do next."

"Looks clear to me."

"Ok, here we go." Ladwick dropped to his knees and fumbled with the lid of a manhole near the gutter. "This should just pop right off."

"I hear footsteps," said Melissa.

"Damn it." He'd tore off most of his fingernails trying to pry up the lid.

A man rounded the corner waving a club. "Don't move."

Ladwick, on his knees, turned toward him uncertain whether to continue with the lid, or cast a protective shield. When the man raised a whistle to his lips, Melissa made a decision for them. She raised the crossbow from under her ragged cloak and fired a bolt into the man's chest. He dropped immediately.

At the same time, the lid came free and Ladwick wrestled it aside.

"It's water ten feet down," he said. "Jump."

She looked at him with wondering eyes. "Sewer water?"

"Really? That's your worry now? Hurry. Let the current take you. Work your way to the right, and feel for a thick rope, a couple hundred yards down. I'll be right behind."

"It's dark," she said, more or less to herself, but she stuck her feet in, balanced with her hands on each side for a moment then dropped out of sight. A splash and a gasp.

He marveled at her faith in him.

He slid into the hole backwards on his stomach, feet feeling for rungs he knew were there. Once in, took a last look, and was dismayed to see the crossbow lying in the street where Melissa had dropped it. Shit. Too late to get it now. He couched low and jostled the cover back into its setting before he too dropped into the dark water.

Within seconds, a boy scurried over the sill of a blown out window, scooped up the crossbow, and disappeared back from where he had come. Another boy reached the man Melissa had killed and took his club. Others arrived to pull the bolt out of his chest, search pockets, and strip off clothing. By the time Lars' men reached the area, the corpse was naked, on its back, oozing blood from the hole in its chest. Small footprints covered the street.

"Ahhhh . . ." He'd forgotten how cold this water got over the winter. And how fast and noisy the current. "Can you hear me?"

"Yes." Her voice echoed faintly from downstream. He made for the wall himself.

"I have the rope," she said. He soon reached her.

"Can you climb?"

"Barely. I pretty much can't feel my legs."

"Let me go up first. He climbed until he reached a trapdoor that opened into an alcove. His hands searched the darkness for the wench he knew was there.

"Hold tight, I'm pulling you up now." He cranked the rope until she reached the edge.

"I wish I wasn't so helpless," she said.

"Not your fault."

He managed to get his arms around her body and rolled her over the ledge onto the dirt floor. They came to rest with him on top of her, quite accidentally. Worried she might think him a cad, he apologized.

"Don't know why you're sorry," she said. "If you want, we

can roll around some more later, but right now I'm freezing."

Ladwick replaced the rope, and closed the trap door. Then led them through a hole in the opposite wall into a room of a house with no roof. The sun was blinding. "We're safe. Just walk normally from here on."

As they passed under a row of mortar-mangled buckthorn trees, he put his arm around her damp shoulders.

They had only been in his house for a few hours, enough to wash, put on dry clothes, and eat, when a frantic Grigg, and a man he introduced as Doth, came to the door.

"You guys gotta go. Lars caught some orphans with a crossbow who say they saw you kill his man. They know who you are and where you live."

"Why am I not surprised?" asked Melissa.

Grigg took Ladwick's arm. "Doth can lead you down the passages under the river to a hideout on the far side. Later, he'll show you a farm where you can buy horses."

Ladwick touched his forehead. "I have to think."

"What's to think? Get across the river, head for the mountains, don't get eaten by Gnolls."

"We can find you a new magic staff," offered Melissa.

"Any chance you arranged this for my benefit?" asked Ladwick, half grinning.

"Sorry, not this time." Grigg nodded toward Melissa. "But hey, now you get to be the new you with someone who won't keep bugging you to be the old you."

Ladwick grabbed his friend in a bear hug. "Catch up to us when its safe?"

"You bet."

Born in Binghamton, NY, **John M. Kuharik** is a 1971 Rider College graduate, an Army veteran, and a career public health retiree. He loves alternate universes, and time travel, and spends ridiculous amounts of time playing fantasy MMORG's. His stories, "Brainboy," "Don't See How It Won't Get Worse," and "Suddenly Tired," have appeared in *The Prairie Light Review*. The first Grigg adventure, "In the Fight For His Life," appeared in *The Digest Enthusiast* book two.

"I've visited other planets, but I've always felt alienated."

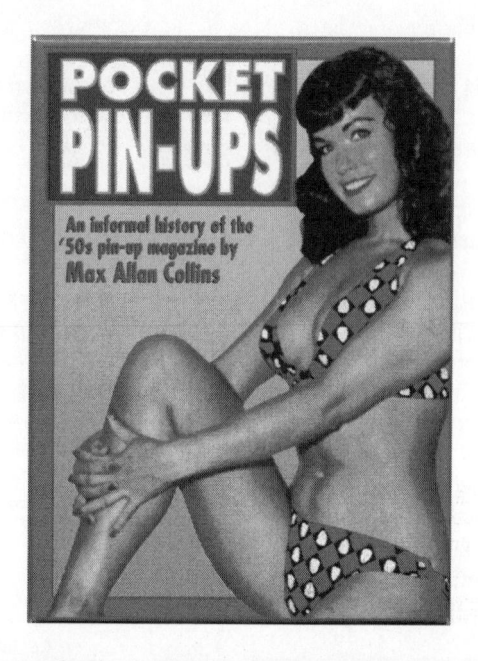

Pocket Pin-Ups Trading Cards
Article by Richard Krauss

Thirty-six is the number of the cards selected for this "informal history of the '50s pin-up magazine" by crime fictioneer Max Allan Collins.

The *Pocket Pin-Ups* trading card set provides high-quality reproduction of a enticing collection of pocket magazine covers from the 1950s. Each card front features a different cover, of which all but four are in full color. Each back includes informative facts and commentary by Max Allan Collins. "Such titles as *He*, *Pose*, *Dare*, *Behind The Scenes*, *Swank*, *Exclusive* and *Reward* moved up to digest or full-size. In some cases, these magazines folded shortly after their size—and price—increased."

Some of the exceptional cover girls featured in these magazines were already Hollywood starlets, but where did the rest of them come from? "The Hollywood PR mills provided many of these lovelies, while others swayed onto the scene from the runways of burlesque."

The opening card of the deck features the cover of *Show* December 1954 with a smiling Betty Page in a skimpy baby blue bikini. "Of [all] these [models] the acknowledged superstar was Betty Page. With one notable blonde Holly-

Card 1: *Show* Dec. 1954 with Betty Page

Card 2: *That Girl Marilyn!* circa 1953

wood exception, the now legendary Miss Page appeared on more covers of pocket pin-up magazines than any other model." She is, of course, followed with the cover of *That Girl Marilyn!* (circa 1953).

The official count of appearances in this particular card set—Betty Page racks up eight while all the others, gorgeous as they may be, only grace a single card cover. They are in alphabetical order: Brigitte Bardot, Candy Barr, Betty Brosmer, Lilly Christine, Yvonne De Carlo, Mara Corday, Dolores Donlon, Anita Ekberg, Marla English, Dixie Evans, Alison Hayes, Arlene Hunter, Joi Lansing, Tina Louise, Jayne Mansfield, Irish McCalla (Sheena), Eve Meyer, Marilyn Monroe, Cleo Moore, Terry Moore, Barbara Nichols, Julie Newmar, Jane Russell, Lili St. Cyr, Maria Stinger, Judy Tyler, Mamie Van Doren and Diane Webber.

Magazine titles represented in the set are: *Bare* (3), *Bold* (6), *Carnival* (2), *Celebrity*, *Chicks and Chuckles*, *Focus* (2), *He*, *People*, *People Today* (5), *Picture Life*, *Quick*, *She* (3), *Show*, *Slick*, *Tempo* (5), *That Girl Marilyn!* and *TV Girls and Gags*.

With only minor wear noticeable on a few covers, and only one with newsdealer markings (card 29: *Chicks and Chuckles* with Betty Page), the quality of the copies of the original magazines selected for reproduction is excellent. And Collins' backside commentary is witty and informative, with loads of factoids on each model's career, mostly on stage or screen.

Produced by Denis Kitchen's Kitchen Sink Press, the cards' production values are top notch. From the quality of reproduction, the consistently even trim, Collins' thorough research, to the sturdy two-piece retail box, this now out-of-print card set is well worth today's going price (about $12) in secondary markets.

Social Intercourse

Engage! Poke a keyboard and make some meaningful interactions on or offline.

The Digest Enthusiast #3 (*TDE3*)
cover by Joe Wehrle, Jr.

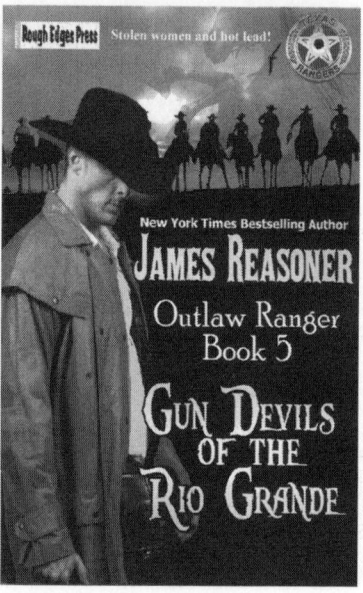

Gun Devils of the Rio Grande
by James Reasoner

    Growth for digests like *TDE* are incremental at best. Every bit of help readers give us and our ilk to help spread the word is greatly appreciated. Long-time supporter Bill Crider wrote about *TDE3* on his Pop Culture Magazine blog: "Of particular interest to me in this issue is Peter Enfantino's summary and rating of every story in *Super-Science Fiction* . . ." and "Steve Carper's article on the digest publications of the stories of Dashiell Hammett . . ." Bill also highlighted our Digest Magazines blog soon after we returned to a schedule of daily posts.

    James Reasoner was in sync with Bill via his Rough Edges blog where he wrote: "Highlights this time around are two pieces by Peter Enfantino . . ." and "Steve Carper's look at the digest appearances of Dashiell Hammett's novels and stories."

    Bill Thom listed *TDE3* for several weeks on his essential PulpComingAtrractions.com weekly announcements, and continues to link to many of our Digest Magazines blog posts.

    Like the amazing Michael Neno, who recently completed work on *The Vicar*, Londoner Sean

Nix Comics' *The Vicar* by Ken Eppstein and Michael Neno

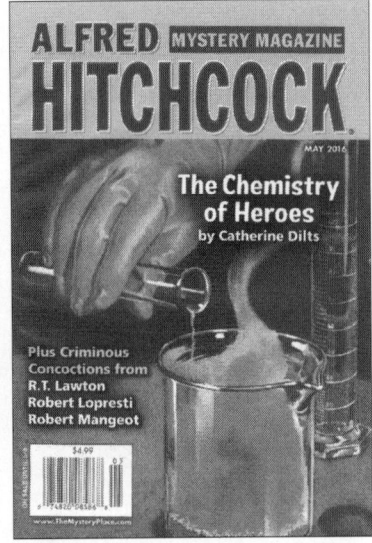

AHMM May 2016 with Robert Lopresti's "Shanks Goes Rogue"

Azzopardi is an avid comic book artist. Check out Sean's work with Daniel Merlin Goodbrey on two volumes of *Necessary Monsters*.

Other blogs we follow include J. Kingston Pierce's The Rap Sheet and Killer Covers. What a nice surprise to discover we made it onto the killercoversoftheweek's blog roll—it least for a moment. That sort of linkage on other blogs helps search engine ranking considerably.

Robert Lopresti, who writes the Leopold Longshanks series, shared our Digest Magazines' post on his first published story in *Mike*

How to Fix Your Novel by Steve Alcorn

Steve & Vicki Ogden's *FAPA*, cover by Joe Wehrle, Jr.

Tapestry of Blood by Ron Fortier

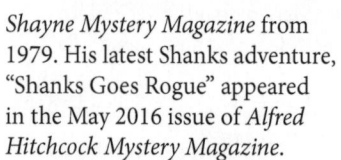

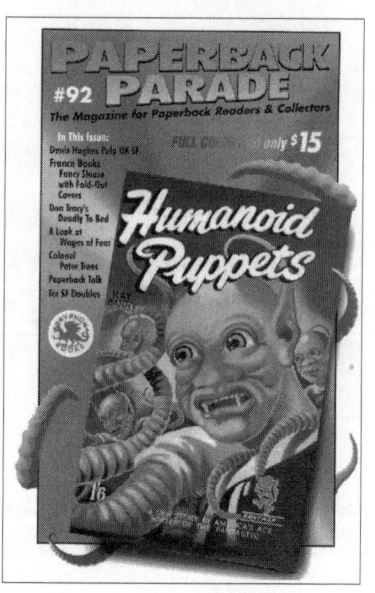

Gary Lovisi's *Paperback Parade* #92

Shayne Mystery Magazine from 1979. His latest Shanks adventure, "Shanks Goes Rogue" appeared in the May 2016 issue of *Alfred Hitchcock Mystery Magazine*.

Airship 27's Captain Ron Fortier mentioned *TDE3* on his weekly Flight Log. If you enjoyed Ron's Brother Bones story in this edition of *TDE* be sure to check out the character's novel series available in print and digital versions with plenty of interior illustrations by Rob Davis.

Gary Lovisi wrote a post about *TDE3* with on Facebook, which read in part: "Each issue is loaded with cool and wonderful articles on all kinds of digest size paperbacks and magazines." Gary, of course, has published the excellent *Paperback Parade* forever. The contents of issue #92 is reviewed in detail on the Digest Magazines blog.

TDE3's listing on Amazon garnered three welcome reviews from Bill Crider, Steve Alcorn and Steve Ogden. Steve Alcorn teaches a collection of fiction writing classes online at writingacademy.com which are very affordable and highly recommended. He also wrote the excellent *How to Fix Your Novel*.

Steve and Vicki Ogden publish *FAPA* aka *Fapazine*, which recently sported a cover by *TDE*'s Joe Wehrle, Jr.

Contributing Editor, D. Blake Werts is an enthusiast of many specialty interests. If you're a fan of mini comics check out his *Copy This!* zine which features news and interviews with newave and indie cartoonists.

Digests on our back cover include:
Ellery Queen June 2007
Suspense #3 Fall 1951
Galaxy Magabook No. 1 1963
Galaxy Novel #19 1953
Spaceway June 1955
Shock Mystery Tales July 1962

Opening Lines
Selected from digests featured in this edition.

"As the cabbie pulled to the curb in front of the only house on the street, something didn't feel right to her."
"The Tell-Tale Cadillac" by Tony W. Brown
Pulp Modern #10, Spring 2016

"The air of the city's cheapest flophouse was thick with the smells of harsh antiseptic and unwashed bodies. The early Christmas snowstorm had driven in every bum who could steal or beg the price of admission, and the long rows of cots were filled with fully clothed figures."
"Badge of Infamy" by Lester del Rey
Galaxy Magabook #1

"It wasn't a lot of money at first, barely-covered enough to buy into a small stakes game."
"Bad Debt" by Jonathan McGoran
Grift Magazine #2 Spring 2013

"During one of their trysts, one of those long lunch breaks they took from the ad agency where they worked, Roger invited Felicia to bring her husband over for a Friday-night cookout."
"The Care and Feeding of Houseplants" by Art Taylor
Ellery Queen March/April 2013

"In a large comfortably furnished office on the twenty-third floor of the Spaceways Building, New York City, Dr. Carl Bressler was addressing an audience of four."
"Spaceways to Venus" by Charles Eric Maine
Spaceway Vol. 1 #1, December 1953

"Just when the idea occurred to her that she was being murdered she could not tell."
"Small Assassin" by Ray Bradbury
Suspense Magazine #1, Spring 1951

"I hadn't been thinking about killing Delwood. Not really. But you know how people sometimes have just had *enough*."
"Rearview Mirror" by Art Taylor
Ellery Queen March/April 2010

"Lurking, that lovely spring day, in the office of Dr. Chalmers, Atworthy College Medical Clinic, there might have been two small spirits of the air, pressed back into the dark shadow behind the door, avoiding as far as possible the warm sunlight which fell gently upon the rug."
Fear by L. Ron Hubbard
Galaxy Novel #29 1954

Printed in Great Britain
by Amazon